Repossession of Property on Mortgage Default

Publishing Company Limited

Repossession of Property on Mortgage Default

*by M.P. Thompson, Professor of Law,
University of Newcastle upon Tyne*

Tolley Publishing Company Limited
A UNITED NEWSPAPERS PUBLICATION

ISBN 1 85190 194 9

First published 1993

A catalogue record for this book is available from the British Library

Published by
Tolley Publishing Company Limited
Tolley House
2 Addiscombe Road
Croydon
Surrey
CR9 5AF
081-686 9141

All rights reserved

© 1993 Mark P Thompson

Printed and bound in Great Britain by
Hartnolls Ltd, Bodmin, Cornwall

Preface

In recent times, there has been a depressing rise in the number of cases where house owners have defaulted on their mortgages with the result that the mortgagee has taken possession in order to enforce its security. This phenomenon has, of course, caused serious social problems for the people who have lost their homes. The wave of repossessions has also had economic implications, the coming on to the market of a considerable number of repossessed houses contributing to the generally depressed state of the housing market.

It should occasion little surprise that this depressing backdrop should also bring to light a number of legal difficulties, there having been in recent times a considerable amount of litigation concerning actions by mortgagees to enforce their securities. This book does not purport to be a general work on the law of mortgages. Rather, it is an attempt to analyse, within a modest compass, the rights and duties of the parties affected by possession proceedings and the subsequent sale of the property and to focus, in particular, on the modern problems that have come to light.

As just mentioned, there have been a number of important recent decisions relating to this area of law. Of these, arguably the most important is that of the Court of Appeal in *Barclays Bank plc* v *O'Brien*. At the time of writing, it is understood that this case is being appealed to the House of Lords and it is hoped that the opportunity is taken to restore clarity to this important area.

I am grateful to the staff at Fourmat for their help in the production of this book and for relieving me of the task of preparing the tables and index. I have tried to state the law as it was on 16 February 1993.

M P Thompson
Newcastle upon Tyne

Contents

Chapter 1:	**Possession actions** 1	
	1. The right to possession 1	
	2. Restrictions on possession 3	
	3. Resisting possession proceedings 22	
	4. Rights and duties upon taking possession 24	
	5. Appointment of a receiver 27	
Chapter 2:	**Third party rights** 30	
	A. *Tenancies* 30	
	1. Leases created before the mortgage 31	
	2. Leases created after the mortgage 33	
	B. *Co-ownership* 36	
	1. Acquisition of an interest in the home 37	
	2. Co-owners and mortgagees: the priority of rights 50	
	3. Limitations on *Boland* 53	
Chapter 3:	**The sale of mortgaged property** 62	
	A. *The power of sale* 62	
	1. The power arising 62	
	2. The power becoming exercisable 65	
	3. Proposals for reform 66	
	B. *The exercise of the power of sale* 67	
	1. The effect of the contract 67	
	2. Duties on sale 68	
	3. Extent of the duty 77	
	C. *Effect of a sale* 81	
	1. Position of purchaser 81	
	2. Proceeds of sale 82	
Chapter 4:	**Priorities of mortgages** 85	
	A. *The law before 1925* 86	
	1. Both mortgages legal 86	

	2.	First mortgage legal; second mortgage equitable 87
	3.	First mortgage equitable; second mortgage legal 92
	4.	Equitable mortgage followed by another equitable mortgage 93
B.		*The law after 1925* 93
	1.	Unregistered land..94
	2.	Registered land 100
C.		*Tacking*..102
	1.	Tacking of further advances....................................103
	2.	Registered land 105

Index 107

Table of cases

Abbey National Building Society v Cann [1991] 1 AC 56, [1990] 1 All ER 1085, [1990] 2 WLR 833 (HL) 32, 50, 52, 54, 88
Agra Bank Ltd v Barry (1874) LR 7 HL 135 93
Alliance Building Society v Pinwill [1958] Ch 788, [1958] 2 All ER 408, [1958] 3 WLR 1 4
American Express International Banking Corporation v Hurley [1985] 3 All ER 564, (1985) 135 New LJ 1034 (DC) 28, 76, 77, 80
Ashley Guarantee plc v Zacaria [1993] 1 All ER 254 3
Atlantic Computer Systems, Re [1992] 1 All ER 476, [1992] 2 WLR 367 (CA)... 6
Att-Gen of Hong Kong v Humphreys Estate (Queen's Gardens) [1987] AC 114, [1987] 2 All ER 387, [1987] 2 WLR 343 (PC) 47
Avon Finance Co v Bridger (1979) 123 SJ 705, [1985] 2 All ER 281 (CA) 58

Bain v Fothergill (1874) LR 7 HL 158 68
Bank of Baroda v Panessar [1987] Ch 335, [1986] 3 All ER 751, [1987] 2 WLR 208 63
Bank of Credit and Commerce International SA v Aboody [1990] 1 QB 923, [1989] 2 WLR 759, [1990] 1 FLR 354 (CA) 58
Bank of Cyprus (London) v Gill [1980] 2 Lloyd's Rep 51 (CA) 73
Bank of Scotland v Grimes [1985] QB 1179, [1985] 2 All ER 254, [1985] 3 WLR 294 (CA) 14, 16
Bannister v Bannister [1948] WN 261, [1948] 2 All ER 133 (CA) 43
Barclays Bank v Kennedy (1989) 21 HLR 132, [1989] Fam Law 143, (1989) 58 P & CR 221 (CA) 59
Barclays Bank v O'Brien [1992] The Times 3 June, [1992] 6 CL 23 (CA) ... 59, 60
Barclays Bank v Taylor [1974] Ch 137, [1973] 1 All ER 752, [1973] 2 WLR 293 (CA) 101, 102
Barclays Bank v Thienel (1978) 122 SJ 472, (1978) 247 EG 385 76
Barclays Bank v Waterson [1989] CLY 2505 19
Basham, Re [1987] 1 All ER 405, [1986] 1 WLR 1498, [1987] 2 FLR 264 46
Bell Street Investments v Wood (1970) 216 EG 585 31
Belton v Bass, Ratcliffe & Gretton [1892] 2 Ch 449 73
Bishop v Bonham [1988] 1 WLR 742, (1988) 132 SJ 933, (1988) 4 BCC 347 (CA) 81

REPOSSESSION OF PROPERTY ON MORTGAGE DEFAULT

Bothe v Amos [1976] Fam 46, [1975] 2 All ER 321, [1975] 2 WLR 838 (CA) ..42
Briggs v Jones (1870) LR 10 Eq 92 88
Bristol Airport v Powdrill [1990] Ch 744, [1990] 2 All ER 493, [1990] 2
 WLR 1362 (CA)...7, 8
Bristol & West Building Society v Henning [1985] 2 All ER 606, [1985] 1
 WLR 778, (1985) 50 P & CR 237 (CA) 53, 54, 55
Britannia Building Society v Earl and Amin [1990] 2 All ER 469, [1990]
 1 WLR 422, (1990) 22 HLR 98 (CA)...34
Bull v Bull [1955] 1 QB 234, [1955] 1 All ER 253, [1955] 2 WLR 78 (CA) 56
Burns v Burns [1984] Ch 317, [1984] 1 All ER 244, [1984] 2 WLR 582 (CA)...41
Buttle v Saunders [1950] WN 255, [1950] 2 All ER 193 71

Castle Phillips Finance Co v Williams [1986] CCLR 13..21
Caunce v Caunce [1969] 1 All ER 722, [1969] 1 WLR 286 52
Centrax Trustees v Ross [1979] 2 All ER 952 13
Chaplin v Young (No 1) (1864) 33 Beav 330 24
Cheah Theam Swee v Equiticorp Finance Group [1991] 4 All ER 989, (1991)
 135 SJ (LB) 205, [1991] NPC 119 (PC) 86
Chhokar v Chhokar (1984) 14 Fam Law 269, (1983) 80 LS Gaz 3243 (CA) 51
China and South Sea Bank v Tan Soon Gin [1990] 1 AC 536, [1989] 3 All
 ER 839, [1990] 2 WLR 56 (PC) 73, 77
Church of England Building Society v Piskor [1954] Ch 553, [1954] 2 All ER
 85, [1954] 2 WLR 952 32
Citibank Trust v Ayivor [1987] 3 All ER 241, [1987] 1 WLR 1157, (1987)
 19 HLR 463...18
City of London Building Society v Flegg [1988] AC 54, [1987] 3 All ER
 435, [1987] 2 WLR 1266 (HL)...55, 56
City Permanent Building Society v Miller [1952] Ch 840, [1952] 2 All ER
 621, [1952] 2 TLR 547 (CA) 32
Clarke v Palmer (1882) 21 Ch D 124 89
Cockburn v Edwards (1881) 18 Ch D 449...25
Coldunell v Gallon [1986] QB 1184, [1986] 1 All ER 429, [1986] 2 WLR
 466 (CA) 59, 60
Colson v Williams (1889) 58 LJ Ch 539..72
Colyer v Finch (1856) 5 HL Cas 905 89
Coombes v Smith [1986] 1 WLR 808, [1987] 1 FLR 352............................47, 48
Corbett v Plowden (1884) 25 Ch D 678...33
Cottey v National Provincial Bank of England (1904) 20 TLR 607.....................90
Crabb v Arun District Council [1976] Ch 179, [1975] 3 All ER 865, [1975]
 3 WLR 847 (CA)...46, 48
Cuckmere Brick Co v Mutual Finance [1971] Ch 949, [1971] 2 All ER 633,
 [1971] 2 WLR 1207 (CA)..72, 73, 77, 79
Cummins, Re [1972] Ch 62, [1971] 3 All ER 782, [1971] 3 WLR 580 (CA).......42

Davey v Durant (1857) 1 De G & J 535 73
De Borman v Makkofaides (1971) 220 EG 805 64

TABLE OF CASES

Densham, Re [1975] 3 All ER 726, [1975] 1 WLR 1519 44
Dixon v Muckleston (1872) LR 8 Ch App 155 87
Dodsworth v Dodsworth (1973) 228 EG 1115 (CA) 49
Downes v Grazebrook (1817) 3 Mer 200 69
Dudley and District Benefit Building Society v Emerson [1949] Ch 707,
    [1949] 2 All ER 252, [1949] LJR 1441 (CA) 33
Duke v Robson [1973] 1 All ER 481, [1973] 1 WLR 267, (1972) 25
    P & CR 21 (CA) 67, 68

Epps v Esso Petroleum Co [1973] 2 All ER 465, [1973] 1 WLR 1071 51
Equity and Law Home Loans v Prestidge [1991] 1 WLR 137, [1991] NPC
    103 (CA) 54, 55, 57, 104
Esso Petroleum Co v Alstonbridge Properties [1975] 3 All ER 358, [1975]
    1 WLR 1474 3
Evans v Bicknell (1801) 6 Ves Jun 174 87
Eves v Eves [1975] 3 All ER 768, [1975] 1 WLR 1338 (CA) 43, 44

Farrar v Farrars (1888) 40 Ch D 395 .... 69, 70, 72
First Middlesbrough Trading & Mortgage Co v Cunningham (1974) 28
    P & CR 69, (1974) 118 SJ 421 (CA) 10, 12
First National Bank v Syed [1991] 2 All ER 250, (1991) 10 Tr LR 154
    (CA) 18, 20, 21, 22
First National Securities v Hegerty [1985] QB 850, [1984] 3 All ER 641,
    [1984] 3 WLR 769 (CA) 56
Four-maids v Dudley Marshall (Properties) [1957] Ch 317, [1957]
    2 All ER 35, [1957] 2 WLR 931 2
Fyfe v Smith [1975] 2 NSWLR 408 25

Garland v Pay (Ralph) & Ransom (1984) 271 EG 106, 116 80
Gissing v Gissing [1971] AC 886, [1970] 2 All ER 780, [1970] 3 WLR 255
    (HL) 38, 39, 40, 41, 42
Goodman v Gallant [1986] Fam 106, [1986] 1 All ER 311, [1986] 2
    WLR 236 (CA) 38
Grant v Edwards [1986] Ch 638, [1986] 2 All ER 426, [1986] 3 WLR
    114 (CA) 38, 40, 43, 45
Grierson v National Provincial Bank of England Ltd [1913] 2 Ch 18 89
Griffiths v Williams (1977) 248 EG 947 (CA) 49

Habib Bank v Habib Bank AG Zurich [1981] 2 All ER 650, [1981] 1 WLR
    1265, [1982] RPC 19 (CA) 47
Habib Bank v Tailor [1982] 3 All ER 561, [1982] 1 WLR 1218, (1982)
    126 SJ 448 (CA) 13, 15
Halifax Building Society v Clark [1973] Ch 307, [1973] 2 All ER 33,
    [1973] 2 WLR 1 11
Hall v Hall [1982] 3 FLR 379 (CA) 41
Hall v Hall [1984] FLR 126 (CA) 37

Hammond v Mitchell [1991] 1 WLR 1127 44
Hastings and Thanet Building Society v Goddard [1970] 3 All ER 954,
  [1970] 1 WLR 1544, (1970) 22 P & CR 295 (CA) 16, 18
Hazell v Hazell [1972] 1 All ER 923, [1972] 1 WLR 301 (CA) 41
Hewitt v Loosemore (1851) 9 Hare 449 92
Hinckley and Country Building Society v Henny [1953] 1 All ER 515,
  [1953] 1 WLR 352 4
Hodson and Howes Contract, Re (1887) 35 Ch D 668 82
Hollington Brothers v Rhodes [1951] 2 All ER 578n, [1951] WN 437,
  [1951] 2 TLR 691 31
Hunt v Carew (1649) Nels 47 46
Huntingford v Hobbs (1992) 24 HLR 652, [1992] NPC 39 (CA) 38
Hussey v Palmer [1972] 3 All ER 744, [1972] 1 WLR 1286 (CA) 41

Inwards v Baker [1965] 2 QB 29, [1965] 1 All ER 446, [1965] 2 WLR 212
  (CA) 46, 49

Jenkins v Jones (1860) 2 Giff. 99 65
Jenroy (Finance) v Stephens (unreported) 28 June 1989 17
Jones (AE) v Jones (FW) [1977] 1 WLR 438 48
Junior Books v Veitchi Co [1983] AC 520, [1982] 3 All ER 201, [1982] 3
  WLR 477 (HL) 80

Keller (Samuel) (Holdings) v Martins Bank [1970] 3 All ER 950, [1971]
  1 WLR 43, (1970) 22 P & CR 68 (CA) 18, 83
Kennedy v de Trafford [1896] 1 Ch 762, (1895-9) All ER Rep 408 72
Ketley (A) v Scott [1981] ICR 241 21
Kings North Trust v Bell [1986] 1 All ER 423, [1986] 1 WLR 119, (1985)
  17 HLR 352 (CA) 58
Kingsnorth Finance Co v Tizard [1986] 2 All ER 54, [1986] 1 WLR 783,
  (1985) 51 P & CR 296 .... 51, 52
Kitney v MEPC [1978] 1 All ER 595, [1977] 1 WLR 981, (1977) 35
  P & CR 132 (CA) 99
Kling v Keston Properties (1985) 49 P & CR 212, (1984) 81 LS Gaz 1683 51
Knight v Lawrence [1991] 01 EG 105, [1991] BCC 411 28

Latchford v Beirne [1981] 3 All ER 705 76
Leeds Permanent Building Society v Kassai [1992] 9 CL 257 19
Lever Finance v Needleman [1956] Ch 375, [1956] 2 All ER 378, [1956]
  3 WLR 72 29
Lloyd, Re [1903] 1 Ch 385 83
Lloyds Bank v Egremont [1990] 2 FLR 351, [1990] FCR 770 (CA) 59
Lloyds Bank v Rosset [1991] 1 AC 107, [1990] 1 All ER 1111, [1990] 2
  WLR 867 (HL) 42, 44, 45, 54

McCarthy & Stone v Hodge (Julian S) & Co [1971] 2 All ER 973, [1971]

TABLE OF CASES

1 WLR 1547, 22 P & CR 1040 103
McHugh v Union Bank of Canada [1913] AC 299 72
Maharaj v Chand [1986] AC 898, [1986] 3 All ER 107, [1986] 3 WLR 440
    (PC) 47, 48, 49
Marriott v The Anchor Reversionary Co (1861) 3 De GF & J 177 25
Marshall v Cottingham [1982] Ch 82, [1981] 3 All ER 8, [1981] 3 WLR 235 28
Martinson v Clowes (1882) 21 Ch D 857 69
Midland Bank v Dobson and Dobson [1986] 1 FLR 171, (1985) 16 Fam
    Law 55, (1985) 135 New LJ 751 (CA) 37, 38
Midland Bank v Farmpride Hatcheries (1980) 260 EG 493 (CA) 52
Midland Bank v Perry [1988] 1 FLR 161, (1988) 56 P & CR 202, (1988)
    18 Fam Law 87 (CA) 59
Midland Bank Trust Co v Green [1980] Ch 590, [1981] AC 513, (1980)
    125 SJ 33 (HL) 31
Mobil Oil Co v Rawlinson (1982) 126 SJ 15, (1982) 43 P & CR 221, (1982)
    261 EG 260 ....18, 83
Mortgage Corporation v Nationwide Credit Corporation [1992] The Times
    27 July 102
Murphy v Brentwood District Council [1991] 1 AC 398, [1990] 2 All
    ER 908, [1990] 3 WLR 414 (HL) 80

Nash v Eads (1880) 25 SJ 95 73
National Bank of Australia v United Hand-in-Hand Band of Hope (1879)
    4 App Cas 391 72
National Provincial Bank of England v Jackson (1886) 33 Ch D 1 93
National Westminster Bank plc v Skelton [1993] 1 All ER 242 18
Northern Counties of England Fire Insurance Co v Whipp (1884) 26
    Ch D 482 90
Norwich and Peterborough Building Society v Steed [1992] 3 WLR 669 (CA) ..57

Oldham v Stringer (1884) 33 WR 251 63
Oliver v Hinton [1899] 2 Ch 264 ....91, 92
Orakpo v Manson Investments [1978] AC 95, [1977] 3 WLR 229, (1977)
    36 P & CR 1 (HL) 55

Paddington Building Society v Mendelsohn (1985) 50 P & CR 244, (1987)
    17 Fam Law 121 (CA) 54
Palk v Mortgage Services Funding [1992] The Times 7 August (CA) 74
Parker v Calcraft (1821) 6 Madd. 11 26
Parker v Watkins (1859) John 153 83
Parker-Tweedale v Dunbar Bank [1991] Ch 12, [1990] 2 All ER 577, [1990]
    3 WLR 767 (CA) 76
Parker-Tweedale v Dunbar Bank (No 2) [1991] Ch 26, [1990] 2 All ER 588,
    [1990] 3 WLR 780 (CA) 83
Pascoe v Turner [1979] 2 All ER 945, [1979] 1 WLR 431 (CA) 49
Payne v Cardiff Rural District Council [1932] 1 KB 241 63

REPOSSESSION OF PROPERTY ON MORTGAGE DEFAULT

Peckham Mutual Building Society v Registe (1981) P & CR 186 4
Perry-Herrick v Attwood (1857) 2 De G & J 21 87
Peter v Russell (1716) 1 Eq Cas Ab 321 87
Pettitt v Pettitt [1970] AC 777, [1969] 2 All ER 385, [1969] 2 WLR 966
    (HL)..38, 39
Pilcher v Rawlins (1872) 7 Ch App 259 92
Predeth v Castle Phillips Finance Co (1986) 279 EG 1355, [1986] 2
    EGLR 144 (CA) 78, 79
Property & Bloodstock v Emerton [1968] Ch 94, [1967] 3 All ER 321,
    [1967] 3 WLR 973 (CA) 67

Quennell v Maltby [1979] 1 All ER 568, [1979] 1 WLR 318, (1978) 38
    P & CR 1 (CA)..3, 34

Refuge Assurance Co v Pearlberg [1938] Ch 687 27
Regent Oil Co v JA Gregory (Hatch End) [1966] Ch 402, [1965] 3 All ER
    673, [1965] 3 WLR 1206 (CA)..5
Reliance Permanent Building Society v Harwood-Stamper [1944] Ch 362...71, 72
Richards v Morgan (1753) 4 Y & C Ex 570 25
Rimmer v Webster [1902] 2 Ch 163 87
Risch v McFee (1990) 61 P & CR 42, [1991] 1 FLR 105, [1991] Fam
    Law 176 (CA) 40
Robertson v Norris (1858) 1 Giff. 421..69
Rochefoucauld v Bousted [1897] 1 Ch 196 43
Rogers' Question, Re [1948] 1 All ER 328 (CA) 40
Royal Trust Bank v Buchler [1989] BCLC 130...6
Royal Trust Co of Canada v Markham [1975] 3 All ER 433, [1975] 1
    WLR 1416, (1975) 30 P & CR 317 (CA) 18
Russel v Russel (1783) 1 Bro CC 269..96

Sandon v Hooper (1843) 6 Beav 246 25
Savage v Dunningham [1974] Ch 181, [1973] 3 All ER 429, [1973] 3 WLR
    471..41
Science Research Council v Nassé [1980] AC 1028, [1979] 3 All ER 673,
    [1979] 3 WLR 762 (HL) 6
Sekhon v Alissa [1989] 2 FLR 94, [1989] Fam Law 355 40
Sharpe, Re [1980] 1 All ER 198, [1980] 1 WLR 219, (1979) 39 P & CR
    459 ....40, 49
Shepard v Jones (1882) 21 Ch D 469...25
Shirlstar Container Transport v Re-Enforce Trading Co [1990] Unreported....3, 17
Standard Chartered Bank v Walker [1982] 3 All ER 938, [1982] 1 WLR
    1410, [1982] Com LR 233 (CA)..73, 74, 76, 78
Steyning and Littlehampton Building Society v Wilson [1951] Ch 1018,
    [1951] 2 All ER 452, [1951] 2 TLR 424 4
Stokes v Anderson [1991] 1 FLR 391, [1991] Fam Law 310, [1991]
    FCR 539 (CA)..44

TABLE OF CASES

Strand Securities v Caswell [1965] Ch 958, [1965] 1 All ER 820, [1965] 2 WLR 958 (CA) 31
Stroud Building Society v Delamont [1960] 1 All ER 749, [1960] 1 WLR 431 34

Target Home Loans v Clothier [1992] The Times 7 August (CA) 18
Taylor v Russell [1892] AC 244 93
Taylors Fashions v Liverpool Victoria Trustees Co Ltd [1982] QB 133n, [1981] 1 All ER 897, [1981] 2 WLR 576 47
Thames Guaranty v Campbell [1985] QB 210, [1984] 2 All ER 585, [1984] 3 WLR 109 (CA) 38
Tinker v Tinker [1970] P 136, [1970] 1 All ER 540, [1970] 2 WLR 331 (CA) ... 40
Tinsley v Milligan [1991] NPC 100, [1991] The Times 22 August (CA) 40
Tomlin v Luce (1889) 43 Ch D 191 79
Town and Country Building Society v Julien (1991) 24 HLR 261 18
Tse Kwok Lam v Wong Chit Sen [1983] 3 All ER 54, [1983] 1 WLR 1349, (1983) 127 SJ 632 (PC) 70, 78
Turnbull & Co v Duval [1902] AC 429 58
Twentieth Century Banking Corporation v Wilkinson [1977] Ch 99, [1976] 3 All ER 361, [1976] 3 WLR 489 64

Ungurian v Lesnoff [1990] Ch 206, [1989] 3 WLR 840, [1990] 2 FLR 299 45

Walker v Hall (1983) 127 SJ 550, (1984) 14 Fam Law 21, (1983) 80 LS Gaz 2139 (CA) 40
Walker v Linom [1907] 2 Ch 104 .... 90, 91
Walthamstow Building Society v Davies (1990) 22 HLR 60, (1989) 60 P & CR 99 (CA) 32
Waring (Lord) v London and Manchester Assurance Co [1935] Ch 310 .... 66, 67, 68
Warner v Jacob (1882) 20 Ch D 220 .... 72, 73
West Penwith Rural District Council v Gunnell [1968] 2 All ER 1005, [1968] 1 WLR 1153 (CA) 2
Western Bank v Schindler [1977] 1 Ch 1, (1976) 32 P & CR 352 (CA) 3, 11
Whitcombe v Minchin (1820) 5 Madd 91 69
White v City of London Brewery Co (1889) 42 Ch D 237 25
White Rose Cottage, Re [1965] Ch 940, [1965] 1 All ER 11, [1965] 2 WLR 337 (CA) 82
Williams & Glyn's Bank v Boland [1981] AC 487, [1980] 2 All ER 408, [1980] 3 WLR 138 (HL) 37, 50, 52, 53, 54, 55, 56
Williams v Wellingborough Council [1975] 3 All ER 462, [1975] 1 WLR 1327 (CA) 69
Willmott v Barber (1880) 15 Ch D 96 47
Woodstead Finance v Petrou (1985) 136 New LJ 188, [1986] CCLR 107 (CA) 21
Wrigley v Gill [1906] 1 Ch 165 (CA); [1905] 1 Ch 241 25

Table of statutes

1914 Bankruptcy Act
s 42 45

1925 Land Registration Act
s 19(1) 51
s 20 101
   (1) 51
s 26(1) 51
s 29 100
s 30 105
s 70(1)(g) 31, 32, 50
   (k) 31, 32
s 106(2) 100, 101

1925 Law of Property Act 29, 84, 86, 93
s 40(1)(2) 96
s 53(1)(b) 38, 43
s 85(2) 25
s 91(2) 63, 74, 75
s 94 104
   (1)(b) 103
   (2)(3) 103
s 97 97-99
s 98 82
s 99 82
   (2)(3) 26
   (13) 30
s 101 .... 35, 62
   (1)(iii) 27
   (3) 65
s 103 .... 27, 62, 65
s 104 66
   (1) 64
   (2) 65

s 105 82
s 109 34
   (2) 28, 80
   (3) 27
   (5) 28
   (8) 27
s 198 98
s 199 52
s 205(1)(xvi) 65

1970 Administration of Justice Act 5, 14, 15, 20
s 36 .... 10-13, 16, 17

1972 Land Charges Act
s 2(4)(i)(iii)(iv) 95
s 4(5) 97-99
s 11(1)-(3)(5) 100

1973 Administration of Justice Act 5, 15, 20
s 8 .... 12, 14, 16, 17

1974 Consumer Credit Act 5, 22
ss 8, 16 19
ss 87, 88 20
s 129(2) 20
s 137 20
s 138(2)-(4) 21
s 140 20

1977 Protection from Eviction Act 4

TABLE OF STATUTES

1977 Rent Act 4, 33, 34

1979 Charging Orders Act 57

1980 Limitation Act 83

1982 Insurance Companies Act 24

1983 Matrimonial Homes Act
s 1(5) 16
s 2(10) 104
s 8(2)(3) 17

1984 County Courts Act
s 21(3) 2

1985 Companies Act
s 425 5

1985 Housing Act
s 452 69
Sch 17 69

1986 Agricultural Holdings Act 4

1986 Building Societies Act 70
s 13(7) 71
Sch 4 71

1986 Insolvency Act
s 8 5

s 11(3)(c)(d) 6, 8
s 14(3) 8
s 15(2) 9
s 17 8
s 334 45
Part 1 5

1987 Banking Act
s 67 23

1988 Housing Act
s 7 ....35, 36
Sch 2 35

1989 Law of Property (Miscellaneous Provisions) Act
s 2 96
s 3 68

1990 Courts and Legal Services Act 2

1992 Social Security Administration Act
s 15A 23

1992 Social Security (Mortgage Interest Payments) Act
Sch 23

Table of statutory instruments

1983 Consumer Credit (Enforcement, Default and Termination Notices) Regulations (SI 1983 No 1561) 20

1986 Building Societies (Supplementary Provisions as to Mortgages) Rules (SI 1986 No 2216) 71

1989 Registration of Title Order (SI 1989 No 1347) 52

1990 Land Registration (Official Searches) Rules (SI 1990 No 1361)
rule 6 100
rule 8 101

1991 High Court and County Courts Jurisdiction Order (SI 1991 No 724)
Art 2(1)(l)..2

1992 Social Security (Claims and Payments) Amendment Regulations (SI 1992 No 1026) 24

Chapter 1

Possession actions

The principal value in being a secured creditor is, of course, the ability to realise the property over which the security is held in order to recover the amount that the creditor is owed. In the context of land, this generally involves an action by a mortgagee ultimately to sell the mortgaged property. As a precursor to this action, it is normally necessary first to obtain possession of the property. This chapter is principally concerned with actions for possession, although some attention is also given to the associated remedy of appointing a receiver.

This chapter is concerned with the rights and duties of the mortgagee and the mortgagor, together with the rights of any spouse of the mortgagor. It should, of course, be appreciated that persons other than the mortgagor may be affected by a possession action of a mortgagee and may be in a position to prevent the success of any such action. The position of third parties is considered in Chapter 2.

1. The right to possession

The general position of a legal mortgagee (and this is also probably true of an equitable mortgagee: see Megarry and Wade, *The Law of Real Property* (5th ed.) pp. 951-952) is that he is entitled to possession. It is a right and not a remedy. This was put in characteristically pungent terms by Harman J, who said:

> "... the right of a mortgagee to possession in the absence of some contract has nothing to do with default on the part of the mortgagor. The mortgagee may go into possession before the ink is dry on the mortgage unless there is something in the mortgage, express or implied, whereby he has contracted himself out of that right." (*Four-maids Ltd* v *Dudley Marshall (Properties) Ltd* [1957] Ch 317 at 320).

As this dictum makes clear, the mortgagee's ability to take possession is, *prima facie*, a right. It is also evident that this right is not unqualified. There may be something in the mortgage that precludes the mortgagee from exercising this right. Moreover, the normal method of taking possession is by obtaining a court order to that effect. Attention will first be given to the question of jurisdiction and then the qualifications to the mortgagee's right to possession will be considered.

(a) Jurisdiction

By statutory provision the great majority of possession actions brought by mortgagees with respect to dwelling-houses must be brought in the county court. Because a possession action is regarded as an action for the recovery of land (see *West Penwith RDC* v *Gunnell* (1968)), the jurisdiction of the county court is governed by what is now s.21(3) of the County Courts Act 1984. The county court has exclusive jurisdiction over actions for possession, brought by a mortgagee, where the land comprises or consists of a dwelling and the property is situate outside Greater London. Formerly the jurisdiction was further limited by reference to the rateable value of the house, but, in furtherance of the general policy of the Courts and Legal Services Act 1990 to extend the jurisdiction of the county court, there is no longer any such limitation (see High Court and County Courts Jurisdiction Order 1991, Art.2(1)(l); (S.I. 1991 No. 724)). Other actions for possession by a mortgagee must be brought in the High Court.

2. Restrictions on possession

As the dictum of Harman J makes clear, the mortgagee is *prima facie* entitled to possession. This right may be qualified by the parties themselves or, alternatively, by statute. These qualifications will be considered in turn.

(a) Qualifications in the mortgage
The mortgage deed may itself qualify the mortgagee's right to possession, for example by containing an express clause to the effect that the mortgagee would not be entitled to possession of the property unless the mortgagor is in default (see e.g. *Shirlstar Container Transport Ltd* v *Re-Enforce Trading Co Ltd* (1990)).

It is possible that it might be found that there has been an implied agreement by the mortgagee that his right to take possession has been restricted. It has been accepted judicially that, in the case of an instalment mortgage, the court will be ready to find an implied term that the mortgagor is to be entitled, as against the mortgagee, to remain in possession until he makes default in repayment – but the mere fact that the mortgage is an instalment mortgage is not, in itself, sufficient to raise such an implication (*Esso Petroleum Co Ltd* v *Alstonbridge Properties Ltd* [1975] 1 WLR 1474 at 1484 *per* Walton J). This approach is characteristic of a judicial reluctance to accept that the mortgagee's right to possession has been abrogated (see also *Western Bank Ltd* v *Schindler* [1977] 1 Ch 1 at 9 *per* Buckley LJ).

In contrast to this, in *Quennell* v *Maltby* [1979] 1 WLR 318 at 322, a wider jurisdiction to refuse possession to a mortgagee was asserted. Lord Denning MR said that "A mortgagee will be restrained from getting possession except when it is sought bona fide and reasonably for the purpose of enforcing its security and then only subject to such conditions as the courts think fit to impose."

This dictum goes far beyond the existing authorities and must be treated with considerable caution. The facts of the case were unusual (see also *Ashley Guarantee plc* v *Zacaria* [1993] 1 All ER 254 at 260, *per* Nourse LJ) and the remarks, which were not supported by the other members of the Court of Appeal, must be read in that factual context (see below, p. 34). It is submitted that there is no such wide-ranging jurisdiction as claimed by Lord Denning.

(b) Attornment clauses

At one time, it was not uncommon for mortgage deeds to contain an attornment clause, whereby the mortgagor attorned, or acknowledged, himself tenant, normally at a nominal rent, to the mortgagee. The reason for this practice was that it was easier for the mortgagee to obtain possession speedily when claiming in his capacity as landlord rather than as mortgagee. This reason no longer exists, although such clauses are sometimes encountered. Where there is such an attornment clause, the mortgagee's right to possession may be restricted by the terms of the clause. Thus if, under the clause, the mortgagee is required to serve a specified period of notice on the mortgagor in order to determine the tenancy, then he will not be entitled to possession until a notice of the proper length has been served (*Hinckley and Country Building Society* v *Henny* (1953)). Although the effect of an attornment clause is to create a relationship of landlord and tenant between the mortgagor and the mortgagee, it has been held that the mortgagor does not acquire the protection afforded to residential tenants under the Rent Acts and the Protection From Eviction Act 1977 (see *Alliance Building Society* v *Pinwill* (1958); *Peckham Mutual Building Society* v *Registe* (1980)), or the Agricultural Holdings Act 1986 (*Steyning and Littlehampton Building Society* v *Wilson* (1951)), although this may, perhaps, be otherwise if the rent reserved is a rack-rent or the attornment contains a term obliging the mortgagor personally to reside in the property (*Alliance Building Society* v *Pinwill* [1958] Ch 788 at 792 *per* Vaisey J).

Because the principal reason for the use of an attornment clause – the availability of a speedy possession procedure – is no longer valid, the inclusion of such a clause in a modern mortgage has been criticised, such clauses being described as entirely obsolete and serving no useful purpose (*Steyning and Littlehampton Building Society* v *Wilson* [1951] Ch 1018 at 1020 *per* Danckwerts J). Such criticism is not, however, wholly justified. Where such a clause may have some practical utility is where the mortgagor assigns the property subject to the mortgage. In such a case, the assignee may be liable upon the covenants contained in the mortgage under the doctrine of privity of estate (see *Regent Oil Co Ltd* v *JA Gregory (Hatch End) Ltd* (1966) (a solus agreement)). For this reason one may still continue to encounter attornment clauses, particularly where commercial property has been mortgaged, despite the fact that the original reason for their use has now become obsolete.

(c) Statutory restrictions
Of considerably more importance than the restrictions imposed by the parties themselves on the mortgagee's right to possession are the restrictions imposed by statute. These are aimed principally at mortgaged properties which include dwelling-houses, and full consideration is given below to the powers of the courts under the Administration of Justice Acts 1970 and 1973, as well as under the Consumer Credit Act 1974.

Corporate mortgagors who have become insolvent are also subject to statutory restrictions.

(i) Corporate mortgagors
Under the Insolvency Act 1986, a procedure exists to appoint an administrator of a company that is in financial difficulties. Under s.8 of the Act, the court may appoint an administrator if it is satisfied that the company is, or is likely to become, unable to pay its debts and considers that the making of an order would be likely to achieve one or more of the purposes listed in the Act. These purposes, which must be specified by the court when making an order, are:
(i) the survival of the company, and the whole or any part of its undertaking, as a going concern;
(ii) the approval of a voluntary undertaking under Part 1 of the Act;
(iii) the sanctioning of a voluntary arrangement under s.425 of the Companies Act 1985 of a compromise or arrangement between the company and any such persons as are mentioned in that section; and
(iv) a more advantageous realisation of the company's assets than would be effected on a winding up.
The effect of an administration order is that a statutory moratorium

on the realisation of the company's assets comes into being. In particular, under s.11(3)(c) of the Act, it is provided that, during the period when an administration order is in force, no steps may be taken to enforce any security over the company's property except with the consent of the administrator and subject (where the court gives leave) to such terms as the court may impose.

When an administration order is in force and a mortgagee seeks to enforce the security by taking possession with a view to selling the property, and the administrator will not consent, then an application must be made to the court to enforce the security. Guidance in respect of the approach to be taken to such applications was given recently by the Court of Appeal in *Re Atlantic Computer Systems plc* [1992] 1 All ER 476 at 501-503. Giving the judgment of the court, Nicholls LJ said:

"(1) It is in every case for the person who seeks leave to make out a case for him to be given leave.

(2) The prohibition in s.11(3)(c) and (d) is intended to assist the company, under the management of the administrator, to achieve the purpose for which the administration order was made. If granting leave to a lessor of land or the hirer of goods (a "lessor") to exercise his proprietary rights and repossess his land or goods is unlikely to impede the achievement of that purpose, leave should normally be given.

(3) In other cases when a lessor seeks possession the court has to carry out a balancing exercise, balancing the legitimate interests of the lessor and the legitimate interests of the other creditors of the company (see Peter Gibson J in *Royal Trust Bank* v *Buchler* [1989] BCLC 130 at 135).

The metaphor employed here, for want of a better, is that of scales and weights. Lord Wilberforce adverted to the limitations of this metaphor in *Science Research Council* v *Nassé* [1980] AC 1028 at 1067. It must be kept in mind that the exercise under s.11 is not a mechanical one; each case calls for an exercise of judicial judgment, in which the court seeks to give effect to the purpose of the statutory provisions, having regard to the parties' interests and all the circumstances of the case. As already noted, the purpose of the power to give leave is to enable the court to relax the prohibition where it would be inequitable for the prohibition to apply.

(4) In carrying out the balancing exercise great importance, or weight, is normally given to the proprietary interests of the lessor. Sir Nicolas Browne-Wilkinson V-C observed in *Bristol Airport plc v Powdrill* [1990] Ch 744 at 767 that, so far as possible, the administration procedure should not be used to prejudice those who were secured creditors when the administration order was made in lieu of a winding up order. The same is true regarding the proprietary interests of a lessor. The underlying principle here is that the administration for the benefit of unsecured creditors should not be conducted at the expense of those who have proprietary rights which they are seeking to exercise, save to the extent that this may be unavoidable and even then this will usually be acceptable only to a strictly limited extent.

(5) Thus it will normally be a sufficient ground for the grant of leave if significant loss would be caused to a lessor by a refusal. For this purpose loss comprises any kind of financial loss, direct or indirect, including loss by reason of delay, and may extend to loss that is not financial. But if substantially greater loss would be caused to others by the grant of leave, or loss which is out of all proportion to the benefit that leave would confer on the lessor, that may outweigh the loss to the lessor caused by a refusal.

Our formulation was criticised in the course of argument, and we certainly do not claim for it the status of a rule in those terms. At present we say only that it appears to us the nearest we can get to a formulation of what Parliament intended.

(6) In assessing these respective losses the court will have regard to matters such as: the financial position of the company, its ability to pay the rental arrears and the continuing rentals, the administrator's proposals, the period for which the administration has already been in force and is expected to remain in force, the effect on the administration if leave were given, the effect on the applicant if leave were refused, the end result sought to be achieved by the administration, the prospects of that result being achieved, and the history of the administration

so far.

(7) In assessing these matters it will often be necessary to assess how probable the suggested consequences are. Thus if loss to the applicant is virtually certain if leave is refused, and loss to others a remote possibility if leave is granted, that will be a powerful factor in favour of granting leave.

(8) This is not an exhaustive list. For example, the conduct of the parties may also be a material consideration, as it was in the *Bristol Airport* case. There leave was refused on the ground that the applicants had accepted benefits under the administration, and had only sought to enforce their security at a later stage: indeed, they had only acquired their security as a result of the operations of the administrators. It behoves a lessor to make his position clear to the administrator at the outset of the administration and, if it should become necessary, to apply to the court promptly.

(9) The above considerations may be relevant not only to the decision whether leave should be granted or refused, but also to a decision to impose terms if leave is granted.

(10) The above considerations will also apply to a decision whether to impose terms as a condition for refusing leave. Section 11(3)(c) and (d) makes no provision for terms being imposed if leave is refused, but the court has power to achieve that result. It may do so directly, by giving directions to the administrator: for instance under s.17 or in response to an application by the administrator under s.14(3), or in exercise of its control of an administrator as an officer of the court. Or it may do so indirectly, by ordering that the applicant shall have leave unless the administrator is prepared to take this or that step in the conduct of the administration.

Cases where leave is refused but terms are imposed can be expected to arise frequently. For example, the permanent loss to a lessor flowing from his inability to recover the property will normally be small if the administrator is required to pay the current rent. In most cases this should be possible, since if the administration order has been rightly made the business should generally be sufficiently viable to hold down current outgoings. Such a term may therefore be a normal term to impose.

(11) The above observations are directed at a case such as the present where a lessor of land or the owner of goods is seeking to repossess his land or goods because of non-payment of rentals. *A broadly similar approach will be applicable on many applications to enforce a security: for instance, an application by a mortgagee for possession of land.* On such application an important consideration will often be whether the applicant is fully secured. If he is, delay in enforcement is likely to be less prejudicial than in cases where his security is insufficient.

(12) In some cases there will be a dispute over the existence, validity or nature of the security which the applicant is seeking leave to enforce. It is not for the court on the leave application to seek to adjudicate upon that issue, unless (as in the present case, on the fixed or floating charge point) the issue raises a short point of law which it is convenient to determine without further ado. Otherwise the court needs to be satisfied only that the applicant has a seriously arguable case." (Italics supplied.)

In addition to the limitation imposed upon the mortgagee's right of possession, when an administration order is in force, the administrator is also empowered to dispose of the property free from the mortgage. Under s.15(2) of the Insolvency Act 1986, in order for the administrator to dispose of the property, he must obtain leave from the court. This will be given if such a disposal is likely to promote the purpose or one or more of the purposes specified in the administration order and it is a condition of leave being granted that the proceeds of sale are applied to discharging the sums secured by the security. Where the proceeds are less than such amount as may be determined by the court to be the net amount which would be realised on a sale of the property in the open market by a willing vendor, then a condition must be included that directs such sums as are necessary to make good the deficiency to the holder of the security.

(ii) Dwelling-houses

Ever since 1970, there has existed statutory jurisdiction allowing a court to postpone the taking of possession by a mortgagee when the mortgaged property includes a dwelling-house. The rationale of this jurisdiction was set out by the Payne Committee in its Report on the Enforcement of Debts (1969 Cmnd. 3909, para. 1386) as being that "[a]ny man's income or earnings can fall suddenly through no fault of his own, and he should be able to look to the courts for any protection he may need against onerous claims arising out of the change in his means". That such protection was necessary was evident from the fact that, without it, the position of the mortgagor when faced with an action for possession by a mortgagee has been described as weak and almost defenceless (*First Middlesbrough Trading Co* v *Cunningham* (1974) 28 P & CR 69 at 71 *per* Scarman LJ). Unfortunately, owing principally to the poor drafting of the relevant legislation, it has been observed, in a penetrating article, that "however clear the goal of this promised land the meanderings of the law towards it have made the wanderings of the children of Israel in the wilderness look almost direct" (Stephen Tromans [1984] Conv 91).

Administration of Justice Act 1970: The main statutory provision is s.36 of the Administration of Justice Act 1970. This provides that:

Where the mortgagee under a mortgage of land which consists of or includes a dwelling-house brings an action in which he claims possession of the mortgaged property, not being an action for foreclosure in which a claim for possession of the mortgaged property is also made, the court may exercise any of the powers conferred on it by subsection (2) below if it appears to the court that in the event of its exercising the power the mortgagor is likely to be able within a reasonable period to pay any sums due under the mortgage or to remedy a default consisting of a breach of any other obligation arising under or by virtue of the mortgage.

(2) The court –
(a) may adjourn the proceedings, or
(b) on giving judgment, or making an order, for delivery of possession of the mortgaged property, or at any time before the execution of such judgment or order, may –
(i) stay or suspend execution of the judgment or order, or
(ii) postpone the date for delivery of possession,

POSSESSION ACTIONS

for such period or periods as the court thinks reasonable.

This section gave rise to two difficulties in terms of its construction, one of relatively minor importance but the second of considerable impact. The first difficulty was whether there was jurisdiction to postpone possession if the mortgagor was not in default. This question arose in *Western Bank Ltd* v *Schindler* (1976). Under the terms of a poorly drafted mortgage, the mortgagor borrowed £32,000 to be repaid in ten years. The loan was secured by a legal charge and an endowment policy which would mature at the end of the ten year period. Although the mortgagor made three payments of interest and three payments of the premium, there was nothing in the mortgage deed which obliged him to do this. Neither payment of interest or of capital could be required until ten years had elapsed. When the mortgagor fell into arrears with the payments under the endowment policy, thereby weakening the security of the mortgagee, the mortgagee sought possession. The main issue in the case was whether the court had jurisdiction under the 1970 Act to postpone possession.

The argument for the mortgagee was that s.36 conferred jurisdiction, *inter alia*, to postpone possession if the mortgagor could, within a reasonable time, pay any sums due under the mortgage, or remedy any default under the mortgage. On the facts of this case, there were no sums due nor any default. Hence, it was argued, there was no jurisdiction under the Act to postpone a possession order. The majority of the Court of Appeal nevertheless held that there was jurisdiction under the Act. This was on the basis that it was considered to be absurd that a mortgagor in default should be in a better position than one who was not. The view was expressed that the effect of the Act was to give the courts a general discretion to postpone possession but, in cases where the mortgagor was in default, that discretion was limited by the criteria set out in s.36. On the facts, however, the court declined to postpone a possession order, although it should be appreciated that the mortgagee would not have had available the statutory power of sale, because the mortgage money had not become due (see below, pp. 63, 64).

The second difficulty with the section was potentially more serious and led to amending legislation. In *Halifax Building Society* v *Clark* (1973) under the terms of an instalment mortgage there was a default clause whereby, in the event of a default in the payment of an instalment, the whole sum payable under the mortgage became due. The result of this clause was that, at the time of the mortgagee's possession action, the arrears were £72.97 and the whole sum due under the mortgage was £1,420.58. Sir John Pennycuick regarded the argument that any sums due under the mortgage meant any instalments due, in contradistinction to the entire redemption moneys, as an impossible construction of the section and held that, as there was no prospect of the mortgagor redeeming the mortgage within a reasonable time, there was no jurisdiction under the Act to postpone possession.

This unfortunate decision, which undermined the aim of the Act, could have been avoided by negating the effect of the default clause, whose only purpose is to trigger the statutory power of sale (see below, pp. 63, 64), by regarding a reasonable period to pay as being the whole period of the mortgage. This approach was indeed adopted by the Court of Appeal in *First Middlesbrough Trading Co Ltd* v *Cunningham* (1974), a case decided the day before the coming into effect of the amending legislation.

Administration of Justice Act 1973: To counter the effect of the decision in *Clark*, the obscurely drafted s.8 of the Administration of Justice Act 1973 was enacted. Under the terms of this section it is provided that:

(1) Where by a mortgage of land which consists of or includes a dwelling-house, or by any agreement between the mortgagee under such a mortgage and the mortgagor, the mortgagor is entitled or is to be permitted to pay the principal sum secured by instalments or otherwise to defer payment of it in whole or in part, but provision is made for earlier payment in the event of any default by the mortgagor or of a demand by the mortgagee or otherwise, then for the purposes of section 36 of the Administration of Justice Act 1970 ... a court may treat as due under the mortgage on account of the principal sum secured and of interest on it only such amounts as the mortgagor would have expected to be required to pay if there had been no such provision for earlier payment.

(2) A court shall not exercise by virtue of subsection (1) above the powers conferred by section 36 of the Administration of Justice Act 1970 unless it appears to the court that the mortgagor is likely to be able to pay any amounts regarded (in accordance with subsection (1) above) as due on account of the principal sum secured, but also that he is likely to be able by the end of the period to pay any further amounts that he would have expected to be required to pay by then on account of that sum and of interest on it had there been no such provision as is referred to in subsection (1) above for earlier payment.

This section has given rise to considerable difficulty in terms of discerning its meaning, the principal difficulty being to determine what, if anything, is meant by the expression "is entitled or is to be permitted ... to defer payment of it in whole or in part ...". The principal difficulty is to determine the date from which payment is to be regarded as being deferred.

In *Centrax Trustees Ltd* v *Ross* (1979) a mortgage provided for the payment of quarterly interest payments on the loan and the date of repayment was set at six months from the date of the mortgage. There was also a clause whereby the whole principal sum became due if the mortgagor got into arrears with his repayments. On this event having occurred, the issue was whether the court had jurisdiction under the legislation to postpone possession. This, in turn, depended upon whether the mortgagor was permitted to defer payment. If so, the amount due was the arrears that had built up; if not, it was the total sum borrowed. Goulding J held that the Act had to be construed liberally and regard had to be had to the position in equity as well as at law. Although the mortgage deed stipulated for repayment after six months, there was sufficient evidence that what was intended was an indefinite loan. As payment could, therefore, be delayed after the six month period and the subsequent calling in of the loan under the default clause meant payment was demanded earlier than was envisaged under the mortgage the court had jurisdiction under the legislation to postpone the possession order, a course which, on the facts, was considered appropriate.

A rather different type of mortgage was considered in *Habib Bank Ltd* v *Tailor* (1982). In this case, Mr Tailor had an agreed overdraft with the bank and this was secured by a mortgage. It was a term of the agreement that the loan could be called in upon demand. On Mr Tailor exceeding his overdraft limit, the bank called in the loan and sought possession of the property. The issue in the litigation was whether the court had jurisdiction under the Administration of Justice Acts to postpone a possession order. The Court of Appeal held that it did not. This was because, under the terms of the mortgage, the mortgagor was not entitled to defer payment. This resulted from the agreement being that the money owed was to be repayable upon demand. There was no provision for payment to occur after that date. The argument that, in every case where the mortgagor was not required to repay the money immediately, he was permitted within the terms of the section to defer payment was regarded as an "impossible construction of the section" ([1982] 1 WLR 1218 at 1215 *per* Oliver LJ). Because there was no prospect of the whole amount borrowed being repaid within a reasonable period of time, it followed that there was no jurisdiction to postpone an order for possession.

Although the decision seems clearly correct on the facts, some discomfort was felt with regard to the reasoning in that it seemed to exclude people who had endowment mortgages from the protection of the Acts (see Stephen Tromans [1984] Conv 91). Under such mortgages the capital sum borrowed is not repayable until a specified period after the execution of the mortgage, when the endowment policy matures. Thereafter, there is no provision for any further delay in repayment. If, as is usual, there is a provision in the mortgage that the whole sum becomes repayable if there is a default in the payments under the endowment policy, then it would seem that the case fell outside s.8 of the 1973 Act, because the mortgagor was not entitled or permitted to defer payment of the principal sum.

This argument was considered but rejected in *Bank of Scotland* v *Grimes* (1985). This case involved an endowment mortgage which was used to finance the purchase of a home. The policy was due to mature in twenty-five years' time and would pay off the capital sum. On default on the payments of the policy the whole sum became payable and, it was argued, the 1973 Act was inapplicable because the mortgagor was not entitled or permitted to defer payment of the capital sum.

The Court of Appeal was conscious that, to accept this argument, would lead to an unfortunate distinction between repayment mortgages and endowment mortgages. Anxious to avoid such a result, *Habib Bank Ltd* v *Tailor* was distinguished as dealing with an entirely different type of case. Being of the view that the wording of the section was impenetrable (see [1985] 1 QB 1179 at 1187 *per* Sir John Arnold P), the court felt free to adopt a purposive approach to its construction. The view was taken that the legislation was intended to provide relief to all mortgagors who got into temporary difficulties with their mortgage repayments, regardless of the type of mortgage that had been used to finance the purchase of the house. Accordingly, it was held that where payment of the capital sum was not expected for a period of twenty-five years, the mortgagor was entitled to defer payment and that the protective jurisdiction of the Acts was available.

The upshot of this rather troubled history is, therefore, that the Acts will apply to all mortgages of domestic property except where it is genuinely envisaged that the money lent is to be repayable in full upon demand.

Practice Direction 1991: When the banks became increasingly involved in the business of providing finance for house purchasing, it was not uncommon for them to use mortgage deeds that had been employed when creating a mortgage to secure an overdraft – the result being that, on the face of it, the capital sum was repayable upon demand. This, however, was not the true basis of the transaction. In response to this, a Practice Direction was issued in 1991. The terms of this direction are as follows:

1. RSC Order 88, r 5(2) requires that in mortgage actions a copy of the mortgage must be exhibited to the affidavit in support of the originating summons, and the original mortgage or charge certificate must be produced at the hearing.
2. Most building society mortgages now incorporate standard mortgage conditions, and in such cases a copy of the relevant conditions must also be exhibited.
3. Some standard forms of building society mortgages are now so

abbreviated that they give no particulars of the amount of the advance, the term of the loan, the rate of interest or the amount of the instalments, but all these matters are defined in the mortgage conditions by reference to the offer letter. Where the offer letter is thus in effect incorporated into the mortgage by reference, that also should be exhibited to the affidavit.

4. Many bank mortgages, although expressed in the usual bank "all moneys" form, are also qualified by an offer letter or other side letter, providing for repayment of the advance by instalments. In *Bank of Scotland* v *Grimes* it was held that in such cases the mortgage may be treated as an instalment mortgage for the purposes of s.36 of the Administration of Justice Act 1970 and s.8 of the Administration of Justice Act 1973. In these cases also the relevant letter should be exhibited to the affidavit in support ([1991] 3 All ER 768).

Parties to the action: The mortgagor must, of course, be made a party to possession proceedings but consideration must also be given to the mortgagor's spouse. Under s.1(5) of the Matrimonial Homes Act 1983, payment of mortgage payments by the mortgagor's spouse, who is entitled under the Act to occupy the dwelling-house, is regarded as being as good as if made by the mortgagor. Formerly, there was a serious practical difficulty for a spouse in exercising the right to take over the mortgage payments, in that the mortgagee was under no obligation to inform the spouse of the possession proceedings, with the result that when this was eventually discovered, the arrears may be such that it was no longer practicable for the spouse to meet the financial obligations (see *Hastings & Thanet Building Society* v *Goddard* (1970)). The position has since been alleviated, to an extent, by statute.

The position is now that where a mortgagee of land that consists of or includes a dwelling-house brings an action for the enforcement of his security, a spouse who is not a party to the action and who is enabled by s.1(5) to meet the mortgagor's liabilities under the mortgage, may, at any time before the action is finally disposed of, apply to be made a party to the action. The spouse is then entitled to be made a party if the court:

(i) does not see special reason against it; and
(ii) is satisfied that the applicant may be expected to make such payments or do such things in or towards satisfaction of the mortgagor's liabilities or obligations as might affect the outcome of the proceedings or that the expectation of it should be considered under s.36 of the Administration of Justice Act 1970.

(Matrimonial Homes Act 1983, s.8(2)).

Provision is also made for the spouse to be notified of the action. This is dependent upon the registration of either a class F land charge or a notice or caution. If such a charge has been registered, then the spouse is entitled to be served with notice of the action (Matrimonial Homes Act 1983, s.8(3)). This requirement means that the mortgagee, when bringing an action for possession, should include with the documentation presented to the court a clear certificate of search. If this is not done, then the applicant must satisfy the court that there are no persons to be notified under the section (*Jenroy (Finance) Ltd* v *Stephens* (June 28, 1989, unreported, Thanet County Court).

The exercise of jurisdiction under the Administration of Justice Acts: Under Order 6, rule 5 of the County Court Rules 1981, when a mortgagee seeks possession of the mortgaged property, he must include in the particulars of claim, *inter alia*, the amount of the periodic payments required to be paid and the amount of any interest or instalments in arrear at the commencement of the proceedings. In terms of this latter requirement, the amount of arrears should be limited to the amount payable if there had not been a default (Administration of Justice Act 1973, s.8) and should not, therefore, include "extras" such as solicitors' costs, fines or deferred interest payments, notwithstanding that such sums are ultimately recoverable (see Parmiter (1992) LSG, April, 29).

Once it is established what sums are due under the mortgage (if there is a genuine dispute as to this, the court will direct an enquiry: *Shirlstar Container Transport Ltd* v *Re-Enforce Trading Co Ltd* (1990)), the question that then arises is whether the mortgagor is likely to be able to pay off the arrears within a reasonable time, while also meeting his continuing obligations under the mortgage. This is an issue of fact and evidence must be adduced as to this issue (see *National Westminster Bank plc* v *Skelton* [1993] 1 All ER 242 at 252, *per* Slade LJ). If the possession order is to be postponed to give the mortgagor time to pay, then the postponement must be for a finite and not an indefinite period (*Royal Trust Co of Canada* v *Markham* (1975)).

In considering this issue, much will depend on the facts of each case. The court will not, however, in assessing the likelihood of the mortgagor's being able to make sufficient payments to justify the exercise of discretion in his favour, take into account vague possibilities of money being forthcoming, such as receiving a legacy or winning the pools (*Hastings & Thanet Building Society* v *Goddard* [1970] 1 WLR 1544 at 1548 *per* Russell LJ), or hopes of lucrative employment in the future (*Town & Country Building Society* v *Julien* (1991) (an unusually large mortgage)). In similar vein, the court will not make an order which the mortgagor cannot afford to pay, or an order that is affordable but will not clear the arrears (*First National Bank plc* v *Syed* [1991] 2 All ER 250 at 255 *per* Dillon LJ). If, however, the mortgagor is himself seeking to sell the property, in order to raise funds to discharge the mortgage, then it is likely that the court will suspend a possession order for a short period to see if such a sale can be effected, it being accepted that an occupied house is a more attractive proposition on the market than one which is standing empty, the mortgagee having taken possession (*Target Home Loans* v *Clothier* [1992] The Times 7 August).

It has also been long established that, if a mortgagee seeks possession, the existence of a counterclaim will not be taken into account in assessing the mortgagor's arrears (*Samuel Keller (Holdings) Ltd* v *Martins Bank Ltd* (1970); *Mobil Oil Co Ltd* v *Rawlinson* (1982). The same is true if the claim is one to a right of set-off: *National Westminster Bank plc* v *Skelton,* above). Thus in *Citibank Trust Ltd* v *Ayivor* (1987), the mortgagor had counter-claimed against the mortgagee in respect of an expert report failing to reveal extensive dry rot. It was held that the amount claimed should be disregarded in deciding whether the mortgagor was likely to be able to pay off the arrears within a reasonable time. Having disregarded that figure, it was calculated that the arrears would be paid off in eight and a half years and this was not considered to be a reasonable period. The only possible exception to this principle is if the claim against the mortgagee is for rescission of the mortgage (*Barclays Bank Ltd* v *Waterson* [1989] CLY 2505 (Manchester County Court)) but, even then, the mortgagor must not subsequently have affirmed the mortgage (*Leeds Permanent Building Society* v *Kassai* [1992] 9 CL 257 (Hastings County Court)).

Consumer Credit Act 1974: An alternative statutory jurisdiction exists, in respect of certain mortgages, for possession to be postponed under the provisions of the Consumer Credit Act 1974. Under ss.8 and 16 of the Act, a consumer credit agreement is a regulated agreement if the loan does not exceed £15,000 and the agreement is not an exempt agreement. Included within the definition of an exempt agreement is a land mortgage where the mortgage has been granted by a local authority or building society or any of the following:
(a) an insurance company;
(b) a friendly society;
(c) an organisation of employers or organisation of workers;
(d) a charity;
(e) a land improvement company; or
(f) a body corporate named or specifically referred to in any public general Act.

It will be noticed that this definition includes neither banks nor finance companies. Mortgages that come within the definition of a regulated agreement are normally second mortgages.

If a mortgagee seeks possession and the mortgage is a regulated agreement, he must first serve a default notice in the prescribed form. The notice must specify the nature of the alleged breach, state if the breach is capable of being remedied and, if so, what action is necessary to remedy it and the date by which it must be remedied, that date being not less than seven days from the service of the notice. If the breach is not capable of being remedied, the notice must state what sum, if any, is required to compensate for the breach and the date by which it must be paid. The notice must also contain information about the consequences of a failure to comply with it (Consumer Credit Act 1974, ss.87 and 88).

It is further provided under the Consumer Credit (Enforcement, Default and Termination Notices) Regulations 1983 (S.I. 1983, No. 1561) that the default notice must give a description of the agreement, the name and postal address of the creditor and the debtor and the term of the agreement that is being enforced. The debtor must also be informed of his right to apply for a time order to be made.

When a mortgagee is seeking possession of the land, the debtor may apply to the court, under s.129 of the Consumer Credit Act 1974, for a time order to be made. Under s.129(2), a time order shall provide for one or both of the following, as the court considers just –
(a) the payment by the debtor or hirer or any surety of any sum owed under a regulated agreement or any security by such instalments, payable at such times, as the court, having regard to the means of the debtor or hirer and any surety, considers reasonable;
(b) the remedying by the debtor or hirer of any breach of a regulated agreement (other than non-payment of money) within such period as the court may specify.

In the case of a regulated agreement where the mortgagor has fallen into arrears, the court's jurisdiction to afford relief to the mortgagor is wider than the alternative jurisdiction under the Administration of Justice Acts, in that there is no reference to the arrears being paid off within a reasonable time. In appropriate cases, therefore, the court can make a time order that effectively reschedules the repayments over the mortgage period (see *First National Bank plc* v *Syed* [1991] 2 All ER 250 at 256 *per* Dillon LJ). In considering whether to make such an order, however, the court should have regard to the circumstances of the creditor as well as the debtor and, in particular, should not make an order that is either beyond the financial means of the debtor, or will be too little even to keep down the accruing interest on the debtor's account (*ibid*).

Section 137 of the Act also gives the court the power to reopen extortionate credit bargains, in order to do justice between the parties. This jurisdiction is not confined to regulated agreements (Consumer Credit Act 1974, s.140), and so exempt agreements are also subject to these provisions. In determining whether or not a credit bargain is extortionate, the court is directed by s.138 of the Act to have regard to certain criteria. These criteria require the court to consider whether the payments required are grossly exorbitant or otherwise grossly contravene ordinary principles of fair trading. In determining these issues, the court must pay regard to such factors as the interest rates prevailing at the time that the credit bargain was made, the age, experience, business capacity and state of health of the debtor at that time and also the degree to which he was under financial pressure at the time, and the nature of that pressure. From the point of view of the creditor, the court is required to have regard, *inter alia*, to the degree of risk accepted by him, having regard to the value of any security provided (Consumer Credit Act 1974, s.138(2), (3) and (4)).

In exercising their jurisdiction under these provisions, the courts have shown themselves to be willing to countenance bargains where the interest rate on the loan is high. Thus, in *A. Ketley Ltd v Scott* (1981), the court refused to reopen as extortionate a credit bargain where the rate of interest was 48% p.a. and, similarly, in *Woodstead Finance Ltd v Petrou* (1985) an interest rate of 42% p.a. was also upheld, despite the terms of the agreement being regarded as "very harsh" (see [1986] CCLR 107 at 114). An important fact in refusing to reopen the transaction was that the debtor had a very poor record as a repayer of debts and, in consequence, the loan arrangement and the rate of interest was normal for a risk of this kind (*ibid.* at p.115). It would seem to be the case, therefore, that the worse the credit repayment record of the debtor, the less chance he will have of persuading the court to reopen the transaction.

It should not be thought, however, that these authorities establish a benchmark of what is an acceptable rate of interest in a credit transaction, so that a bargain where the rate of interest does not exceed 48% will invariably be regarded as not being extortionate. This point was made clear in *Castle Phillips Finance Co Ltd v Williams* ([1986] CCLR 13 at 20 *per* Dillon LJ), where the view was expressed that an interest rate of 48% p.a. was arguably extortionate, particularly given that the creditor had ample security for its loan. Again, in *First National Bank plc v Syed* (1991), a credit agreement which provided for the payment of compound interest with monthly rests, with the result that the burden of repayment increased considerably as soon as there were arrears, was considered to be arguably extortionate.

The *Syed* case demonstrates also the problems that can face a borrower in seeking to have the credit agreement reopened. In that case, although the Court of Appeal felt there to be an arguable case that the credit agreement was extortionate, it also took the view that the possession proceedings had been pending for sufficiently long a period without this point having been taken that it would not be right to remit the case to a lower court for this issue to be determined. It was also recognised, however, that, in many mortgage possession cases, the mortgagor will appear unrepresented to argue that he should be given more time before being evicted (see [1991] 2 All ER 250 at 251 *per* Dillon LJ). It may then transpire that an arguable case, that the credit agreement was extortionate, has never been raised. The only palliative to this, when the mortgagor is unrepresented, is that it is open to the court to address this matter on its own initiative (*ibid.* at p. 252). Where the mortgagor is represented, however, then attention should be given to the issue of whether a case could be made that the credit agreement should be reopened, under the Consumer Credit Act, as being an extortionate credit agreement.

3. Resisting possession proceedings

As has been seen, there are a number of possible statutory provisions that are potentially of use to a mortgagor in order to prevent the mortgagee from obtaining possession of the property. The success of any such argument will depend, primarily, of course, on sufficient resources being available to satisfy the demands of the mortgagee. Various avenues can be explored by the mortgagor to prevent the house from being repossessed and, in this section, some attention will be given to those possibilities.

(a) Debt rescheduling
If the mortgagor is experiencing difficulties in meeting his mortgage

obligations, it is sensible for him to discuss with the mortgagee a scheme whereby the loan is voluntarily rescheduled, often by extending the period of the loan. Because of the high number of mortgage repossessions that have been taking place, with the consequent social and economic problems that arise, there is evidence that the main lending institutions may be prepared to react sympathetically to a realistic proposal for a rescheduling of the mortgage repayments. Predictably enough, the approach of lending institutions differs (see the survey by Stephen Gold (1989) 139 NLJ 249), but it would always seem sensible for this potential option to be explored.

If a serious proposal is to be made, it is sensible for the mortgagor to approach the lending institution to seek to arrange such an agreement, rather than simply default on the repayments. Where there has been default, there is some variation in the practices of lenders as to how quickly the lender will make contact with the borrower with regard to this (see Stephen Gold (1992) 142 NLJ 342) and, the longer the delay, the greater will be the accumulated arrears, with the result that a rescheduling may be more difficult to negotiate.

(b) Social security

As part of an attempt to renegotiate the mortgage payments, an offer can be made to the mortgagee that it accept only interest repayments for a period of time. If this is acceptable, and the mortgagor is in receipt of social security, then his social security payments will include an amount to cover his mortgage interest payments. Payments in respect of interest under a mortgage can be directed to be paid directly to the mortgagee (Social Security Administration Act 1992, s.15A, inserted by Social Security (Mortgage Interest Payments) Act 1992, Sched.), thereby ensuring that such payments are actually received by the lender, and therefore making such an arrangement more attractive to the mortgagee.

For social security payments to be directed in this way, the mortgagee must be a qualified lender. The list of qualified lenders includes building societies, authorised institutions within the meaning of the Banking Act 1987, to which s.67 of that Act applies, any body carrying out insurance business under the Insurance

Companies Act 1982, various local authorities and the Housing Corporation (*ibid.*; Social Security (Claims and Payments) Amendment Regulations 1992, S.I. 1992 No. 1026).

(c) Mortgage rescue schemes
As part of the Government's response to the high level of mortgage repossessions, provision was made, as outlined above, for social security payments to be payable directly to qualified lenders. In addition to this, building societies were encouraged to participate in mortgage rescue schemes. The essence of these schemes is that the mortgaged property is sold to the Housing Corporation, the finance being provided by a low interest loan to the Corporation, the society retaining an equitable interest in the property, which will then be sold after a specified period of time. In that period, the mortgagor retains possession of the property as the tenant of the Corporation, and thus is not rendered homeless. At present, there is little evidence to suggest that such schemes are having much effect in stemming the tide of repossessions, but, again, it is a possibility that should be explored with the mortgagee.

4. Rights and duties upon taking possession

Having considered the restrictions placed upon a mortgagee as regards his taking possession of the mortgaged property, it is now necessary to consider the rights and duties of a mortgagee who has taken possession.

(a) Liabilities
A mortgagee who takes possession is commonly said to be liable to the mortgagor on the basis of wilful default. This means that "he is accountable to the owner of the equity of redemption for everything which he either has received or might have received, or ought to have received, while he continued in such possession" (*Chaplin* v *Young (No.1)* (1864) 33 Beav 330 at 337-338 *per* Sir John Romilly MR).

A good illustration of this principle is provided by the leading case of *White* v *City of London Brewery Co Ltd* (1889). In this case, the mortgagees, who were brewers, had taken possession of the property and had let it, the lease including a provision that the tenant should purchase only the mortgagee's beer. It was held that the mortgagee was liable to account to the mortgagor for the difference in the rental that could have been obtained had the premises been let as a free house, rather than as a tied house. Consistent with this general principle, if the mortgagee occupies the property himself, then he is liable to pay an occupation rent (*Shepard* v *Jones* (1882) 21 Ch D 469 at 475 *per* Sir George Jessel MR), although no rent is payable if the condition of the property is such that it cannot be said to have a rental value (*Fyfe* v *Smith* [1975] 2 NSWLR 408). Again, a mortgagee in possession is entitled to continue to run a business, but must do so as a prudent man of business and must not engage in hazardous or speculative endeavours (*Marriott* v *The Anchor Reversionary Co* (1861) 3 De GF & J 177 at 186 *per* Lord Westbury LC).

(b) Repairs and improvements
Although a mortgagee in possession is not impeachable for waste (Law of Property Act 1925, s.85(2)), he is required to effect necessary repairs to the property (*Richards* v *Morgan* (1753)). He is, moreover, permitted to effect reasonable improvements to the property (see *Shepard* v *Jones* (1882) 21 Ch D 469 at 480-481 *per* Brett LJ) but if any purported improvements are effected which are not considered to be reasonable, and are done without the mortgagor's consent, then the mortgagee will be liable (*Sandon* v *Hooper* (1843)).

(c) Rents and profits
The mortgagee in possession may first deduct expenses and then what remains goes against the payment of interest and principal (*Cockburn* v *Edwards* (1881) 18 Ch D 449 at 146 *per* Sir George Jessel MR). He is not, however, obliged to use the monies received towards the payment of the principal, because he "is not obliged to accept payment by driblets" (*Wrigley* v *Gill* [1905] 1 Ch 241 at 254 *per* Warrington J). If the mortgagee in possession has notice of a

subsequent incumbrancer, then he is accountable to him in respect of any surplus funds (*Parker* v *Calcraft* (1821)).

The source of any rent is obviously from a tenancy. It may be important to distinguish, however, between a tenancy that was created prior to the mortgage and one which was created subsequent to it. In the case of tenancies created before the mortgage, such tenancies are, in principle, binding upon the mortgagee and he should simply direct that the rent be paid directly to him. If, however, the tenancy was created after the mortgage, by the mortgagor, it is important to establish whether the mortgagor's power of leasing had been excluded by the mortgage deed. If, as is usually the case, the power of leasing had been excluded, then any tenancy that has been created by the mortgagor will not bind the mortgagee. He is nevertheless entitled to the rent as representing the mesne profits from the occupation of the land. Some care is necessary, however, in the manner adopted of receiving such payment. If the rent is collected directly from the tenant, then it is likely that the mortgagee will be regarded as having adopted the tenancy. If this occurs, the mortgagee may subsequently find it difficult to obtain possession of the property, as against the tenant (see pp. 34, 35). The safer practice is, therefore, to appoint a receiver and direct that the rent be paid to him, while also making it clear that the tenancy has not been adopted.

It is open to a mortgagee in possession to create certain leases, as authorised by s.99(2) and (3) of the Law of Property Act 1925. These leases, in the case of mortgages made after 1925, are agricultural or occupational leases not exceeding 50 years, or business leases not exceeding 999 years. The lease must be made to take effect in possession not later than twelve months after its date; shall reserve the best rent reasonably obtainable, without taking a fine; shall contain a covenant by the lessee to pay rent with a condition of re-entry on the rent not being paid within time therein specified not exceeding thirty days. A counterpart of any such lease must be executed by the lessee and served on the lessor.

Where the mortgagee has taken possession and it is apparent that the property will not be sold for an extended period of time, then the mortgagee may come under a duty to lease the property (see Sweet and Maxwell's *Conveyancing Practice* para. 11.019). In the case of an occupational tenancy, the mortgagee should create an assured shorthold tenancy, to avoid conferring upon the tenant security of tenure.

5. Appointment of a receiver

In the light of the obligations imposed upon a mortgagee who goes into possession of mortgaged property, a more attractive option that is open to the mortgagee, particularly when the property is not to be sold for any appreciable period of time, is to appoint a receiver. The general power to appoint a receiver is now governed by the provisions of the Law of Property Act 1925.

Under s.101(1)(iii) of the Act, the mortgagee only has the power to appoint a receiver if the mortgage has been created by deed and the mortgage money is due. Thereafter, under s.109 of the Act, the power to appoint is only exercisable if the criteria regulating the exercise of the power of sale, laid down in s.103 of the Act, are satisfied (see pp. 65, 66). The appointment is then required to be made in writing. If the mortgagee has taken possession of the property, there is nothing to stop him from subsequently appointing a receiver and, if he does so, he will be regarded as having given up possession (*Refuge Assurance Co Ltd* v *Pearlberg* (1938)).

After a receiver has been appointed under the statutory provisions, he is empowered to demand and recover all the income of which he is appointed receiver, by an action for distress, or otherwise, in the name either of the mortgagor or the mortgagee, to the full extent of the estate or interest that the mortgagor could dispose of, and to give effectual receipts for the same, and to exercise any powers which may have been delegated to him by the mortgagee under the Act (Law of Property Act 1925, s.109(3)). Section 109(8) of the Act then directs how the income received by the receiver is to be applied. This is:
(i) in discharge of all rents, taxes, rates and outgoings whatever affecting the mortgaged property; and
(ii) in keeping down all annual sums or other payments, and the interest on all principal sums, having priority to the mortgage

in right whereof he is receiver; and
(iii) in payment of his commission, and of the premiums on fire, life, or other insurances, if any, properly payable under the mortgage deed or under this Act, and the cost of executing necessary or proper repairs directed in writing by the mortgagee; and
(iv) in payment of the interest accruing in respect of any principal money due under the mortgage; and
(v) in payment in or towards discharge of the principal money if so directed in writing by the mortgagee;
and shall pay the residue, if any, of the money received by him to the person who, but for the possession of the receiver, would have been entitled to receive the income of which he is appointed receiver, or who is otherwise entitled to the mortgaged property.

The commission to which the receiver is entitled is defined in s.109(5) as being such rate, not exceeding 5% on the gross amount of all money received, as is specified in his appointment, or, if no such sum is specified, a rate of 5% on the gross amount, or such other rate as the court thinks fit to allow, on application being made by him for that purpose. If there is no specified sum, then the receiver can charge a gross rate of 5% without having to apply to the court; he need only apply if he seeks a different rate (*Marshall* v *Cottingham* [1982] Ch 82. See pp. 87-88 *per* Megarry V-C, on the problems of punctuation caused by this section).

(a) Agency
The principal advantage of appointing a receiver, from the point of view of the mortgagee, is that under s.109(2) of the Law of Property Act 1925, a receiver appointed under the Act is deemed to be the agent of the mortgagor. The main effect of this provision is that the receiver and not the mortgagee is liable to the mortgagor in respect of negligent management of the property (see, for example, *Knight* v *Lawrence* (1991): failure to trigger rent review clauses in leases), unless the receiver is acting under the directions of the mortgagee (see *American Express International Banking Corp* v *Hurley* [1985] 3 All ER 564 at 568 *per* Mann J). On any appointment of a receiver

which is not made under the Act, the receiver is likely to be held to be the agent of the mortgagee (see *Lever Finance Ltd* v *Needleman* [1956] Ch 375 at 382-383 *per* Harman J).

In addition to being relieved from the potentially onerous liability of a mortgagee in possession, the appointment of a receiver has another practical advantage from the standpoint of the mortgagee. If an unauthorised tenancy has been created by the mortgagor, the receipt of rent from the tenant by the mortgagee carries the risk that the tenancy will be held to have been adopted (see pp. 34, 35). This may cause subsequent difficulties in obtaining possession, as against the tenant. If, instead, the rent is collected by a receiver appointed under the Act, this, in itself, will not mean that the mortgagee is considered to have adopted the tenancy (*Lever Finance Ltd* v *Needleman*, above, at p. 382).

In conclusion, therefore, it can be said that if a mortgagee is not minded to sell the property for any considerable period, but wishes to safeguard his security under the mortgage, the appointment of a receiver will normally be a more attractive option than the taking of possession himself.

Chapter 2

Third party rights

For a mortgagee to be able to obtain possession, there must be no adverse interests – which themselves confer a right of occupation – that are binding upon him. The rights which are most likely to affect him are those of tenants and of co-owners. In the case of co-owners' rights, difficult problems can arise in ensuring that requisite consents to the mortgage have been obtained and that any such consents are not liable to be nullified by a vitiating factor, such as undue influence.

A. Tenancies

Under s.99 of the Law of Property Act 1925, both the mortgagor and the mortgagee have the power to create certain leases, as authorised by the Act. This power exists only if and so far as a contrary intention is not expressed in the mortgage deed or otherwise in writing (LPA 1925, s.99(13)). In practice, the mortgagor's power to create tenancies is routinely excluded by the mortgage deed. The issues that arise are (i) what tenancies can be binding on a mortgagee, and (ii) the effect of unauthorised tenancies. Consideration will first be given to the situation where a lease was created before the grant of the mortgage, and secondly to a lease that was created subsequently.

THIRD PARTY RIGHTS

1. Leases created before the mortgage

Where a lease has been created before the mortgage, the question of whether it will be binding upon the mortgagee depends upon whether the lease is legal or equitable and, also, whether or not title is registered.

(a) Legal leases
If the lease is legal, and title to the land is unregistered, then it will be binding upon the mortgagee as a matter of general principle. If title is registered, however, the position is less straightforward. If the lease is for a period of less than 21 years, then it takes effect as an overriding interest under s.70(1)(k) of the Land Registration Act 1925. Where the lease is for a period of over 21 years then, first, it should now be registered with its own substantive title and, second, should also be noted on the freehold title. If the lease has not been registered but, as is likely, the tenant is in actual occupation of the property, then the lease would take effect as an overriding interest under s.70(1)(g) of the Act and thus bind the mortgagee. If the tenant is not in actual occupation, however, perhaps because he has allowed a relative to occupy the property rent free, then the lease will not be binding upon the mortgagee (cf *Strand Securities Ltd* v *Caswell* (1965)).

(b) Equitable leases
If the lease that has been created is an equitable lease, then, in the case of unregistered land, it must be registered as a class C(iv) land charge if it is to be binding upon a subsequent mortgagee. If it has not been so protected then it will not be binding on him, regardless of whether the mortgagee knows of the tenancy or if the tenant is in possession of the property (see *Hollington Brothers* v *Rhodes* (1951); *Midland Bank Trust Co Ltd* v *Green* (1980)). If the tenant has gone into possession and paid rent, however, his position is relatively secure because, although the equitable tenancy will be void for non-registration, there will be a legal periodic tenancy by implication which will be binding on the mortgagee (see *Bell Street Investments Ltd* v *Wood* (1970)). Where title is registered, the posi-

tion is more straightforward. An equitable tenant for a term of less than 21 years does not have an overriding interest under s.70(1)(k) of the Land Registration Act 1925 (*City Permanent Building Society* v *Miller* (1952)) but, if in actual occupation, will have an overriding interest under s.70(1)(g) of the Act.

(c) Tenancies by estoppel
Until quite recently, there existed a potentially serious trap for mortgagees. This trap concerned a situation where a purchaser was buying property with the aid of a mortgage and purported to create a tenancy before the completion of the purchase. Because, at the time that the purchaser purported to create the lease he had no legal estate, the tenancy took effect as a tenancy by estoppel. On the completion of the contract of sale, the purchaser acquired the legal estate and, under the doctrine of feeding the estoppel, the tenant automatically acquired a legal tenancy. Although the mortgage was executed contemporaneously with the conveyance, it was held that, as a matter of legal theory, there was a *scintilla temporis* between the vesting of the legal title in the purchaser and the acquisition of the legal charge by the mortgagee. In that split second, the tenancy by estoppel became a legal lease and was thus binding on the mortgagee (see *Church of England Building Society* v *Piskor* (1954)). This reasoning, while logical, was manifestly inconvenient and has now been rejected by the House of Lords (*Abbey National Building Society* v *Cann* (1990)), so that, in the situation described above, the mortgagee would now have priority.

(d) Subsequent mortgages
A situation where a mortgagee is most at risk of being bound by a pre-existing tenancy is when the mortgage is not contemporaneous with the purchase of the property. If such a mortgage is by way of re-mortgage, however, then it may still be possible that the tenancy will not be binding on the mortgagee. In *Walthamstow Building Society* v *Davies* (1990), a mortgage was created which excluded the mortgagor's power of leasing. Nevertheless, the mortgagor proceeded to create a tenancy of the property. It was then discovered that the mortgage omitted to mention that it was a mortgage under the

MIRAS scheme. To rectify that omission the original mortgage was discharged and a new mortgage created which contained reference to this. When the mortgagee sought possession of the property, the tenants argued that, as their tenancy was in existence before the creation of the new mortgage, it was binding on the mortgagee.

This argument was, not surprisingly, rejected. It was held that the new mortgage was effectively a substitute for the previous one and that, accordingly, there was no change in priorities. A matter that was left open, however, was as to the position if a different mortgagee had been involved, the money advanced being used to discharge the first mortgage. It is suggested that, in this situation, the solution will depend upon the circumstances surrounding the second mortgage. If what occurs is simply that the mortgage is transferred from the first mortgagee to the second, then the position would seem to be the same as in the case itself. Similarly, if it is a term of the second mortgage that the money borrowed is to go towards paying off the original mortgage, then that mortgagee will be subrogated to the rights of the first mortgagee (see also p. 55). Where neither of these events occurs, however, it is thought that the tenancy will be binding on the later mortgagee.

2. Leases created after the mortgage

Where a lease has been created after the mortgage, its effect on the mortgagee will depend upon whether or not the mortgagor's power of creating leases has been excluded by the mortgage deed.

(a) Unauthorised leases

If, as is usual, the power of the mortgagor to grant leases has been excluded then, while the lease is fully binding as between the mortgagor and the tenant, it will not bind the mortgagee, who will be able to obtain possession as against the tenant (see *Corbett* v *Plowden* (1884) 25 Ch D 678 at 681 *per* Lord Selborne LC; *Dudley and District Building Society* v *Emerson* (1949)). Neither is the position of the tenant improved if the original unauthorised contractual tenancy has ended and he now holds as a statutory tenant under the Rent

Acts. The position remains that the mortgagee is entitled to possession of the property (*Britannia Building Society* v *Earl* (1990)).

There are two qualifications to this proposition. The first is that the action for possession brought by the mortgagee must not be a collusive one with the mortgagor. In *Quennell* v *Maltby* (1979), Mr Quennell owned a house which was subject to a small mortgage in favour of a bank. Although the power of leasing had been excluded, he created tenancies in favour of students. He could not obtain possession of the house from them, as they were protected under the Rent Act. Wishing to sell the house with vacant possession, he approached the bank and asked it to evict the tenants, the tenancies not being binding upon it. As the bank was of the view that its security was adequately protected, it declined. Mrs Quennell then redeemed the mortgage, thereby causing the mortgage to be transferred to her. She then sought possession against the students.

The action, not surprisingly, failed. Lord Denning MR asserted a wide ground for the decision. In his view, a mortgagee could only obtain possession if the purpose of so doing was to protect his security. However, this view is inconsistent with the long established position that the taking of possession by the mortgagee is a right and not a remedy (see pp. 1, 2) and, consequently, the majority ground for the decision, that the action was actually a collusive one whereby the landlord was effectively seeking possession, and so could not therefore be allowed to succeed, is to be preferred.

The second qualification is that the mortgagee must take care not to adopt an unauthorised tenancy. In *Stroud Building Society* v *Delamont* (1960) a mortgagor created an unauthorised tenancy. Sometime later he was adjudicated bankrupt. The mortgagee then served a notice to quit on the tenant, but this was not complied with. Instead, for a period of some months, the rent was paid to the mortgagor's trustee in bankruptcy. The mortgagee then appointed a receiver under s.109 of the Law of Property Act 1925 and the tenant was instructed to pay the rent to the receiver. Later still, the mortgagee wrote to the tenant informing her that the terms of the tenancy, which she held as tenant of the mortgagee, were the same as those in the original lease. The question which then arose was whether the mortgagee was entitled to possession as against the tenant.

Cross J held in favour of the tenant. He accepted that the original tenancy between the mortgagor and the tenant was void against the mortgagee who could, therefore, have treated the tenant as a trespasser. On the facts of the case, however, the conduct of the mortgagee was sufficient to amount to an adoption of the tenancy, thereby creating a new relationship of landlord and tenant between itself and the tenant.

It was pointed out, however, that the appointment of a receiver who will then accept rent from a tenant will not, of itself, amount to the adoption of the tenancy. The receiver who is appointed acts as the agent of the mortgagor, although the income that is then received is not paid to the mortgagor. Rather it is utilised in meeting the outgoings on the property and meeting the obligations under the mortgage. Where there is an unauthorised tenancy, therefore, the mortgagee should exercise care if he wants to receive rent in order to meet the mortgagor's financial commitment to him. He should not receive rent directly from the tenant but, instead, should appoint a receiver and direct that the rent be paid to the receiver, while also making it clear that he does not accept the tenancy.

(b) Authorised tenancies

If the mortgage deed does not exclude the mortgagor's power to let, then any mortgages that he creates will be binding upon the mortgagee. Such a mortgage would be unusual.

It is now possible, however, for a mortgagee to allow certain lets to be created without jeopardising his ability to obtain possession in order to realise his security.

Under s.7 of and Schedule 2 to the Housing Act 1988, a new ground for possession is established in the case of tenancies within the Act. Under these provisions, the court must order possession if the dwelling-house is subject to a mortgage granted before the beginning of the tenancy and –

(a) the mortgagee is entitled to exercise a power of sale conferred upon him by the mortgage or by s.101 of the Law of Property Act 1925; and
(b) the mortgagee requires possession of the dwelling-house for the purpose of disposing of it with vacant possession in exer-

cise of that power; and
(c) notice was served upon the tenant prior to the creation of the tenancy that possession could be recovered under this ground, or the court is satisfied that it is just and equitable to dispense with the requirement of notice.

Various points can be made about the operation of these provisions. First, if the mortgage is unauthorised, then the mortgagee's right to possession is unaffected by the 1988 Act. Second, if the mortgagee is prepared to allow the mortgagor to grant tenancies, care should be taken to ensure that possession can be recovered under the Act. This can be done by including a clause in the mortgage which permits tenancies to be created but only on the basis that the relevant notice is served upon the tenant prior to the creation of the tenancy. Alternatively, if the mortgage contains an absolute bar against the creation of tenancies, but the mortgagor approaches the mortgagee for his consent to the creation of a tenancy, then that consent can safely be given if the giving of the requisite statutory notice to the tenant is insisted upon. In this way, if the mortgagor has to vacate the property for a certain period, for example for employment reasons, a tenancy can be created, without endangering the mortgagee's right to possession, should that course of action become necessary.

As a final observation on the position of tenants, if the mortgagor is himself a tenant of the property, then he is not entitled to security of tenure under s.7 of the Housing Act 1988. This provision is included in the Act to enable mortgagees who have lent money on the security of a lease to exercise their right to possession in the normal way.

B. Co-ownership

The ability of a mortgagee to obtain possession of the mortgaged property may be significantly affected by the existence of co-owners in the property, in that a co-owner may have rights which have priority over those of the mortgagee. This matter raises a number of issues. First, consideration must be given to how a person can acquire a beneficial interest in property. Second, the question of the circumstances when such a beneficial interest may be binding on a mortgagee must be addressed, together with the problems associated with consents to a mortgage.

1. Acquisition of an interest in the home

The most common type of situation where difficulties can arise for mortgagees is where there is sole ownership of the legal title but it is subsequently asserted that there is beneficial co-ownership. It is then further claimed that that beneficial interest has priority over the mortgage created by the legal owner, with the result that the mortgagee cannot obtain possession against the equitable co-owner (see *Williams & Glyn's Bank Ltd* v *Boland* (1980), considered at p. 50).

In such cases, the court will consider carefully whether there is in fact co-ownership; it will not simply accept the word of the mortgagor and his partner that that is the case. The reason for this scepticism is that, if the relationship between the two has not broken down, the mortgagor will benefit from a decision in favour of his partner, in that there is little point in the mortgagee obtaining possession as against the mortgagor if it cannot also obtain possession as against his partner. The mortgagor in this situation will therefore be able to retain possession of the property despite being in default on the mortgage. Consequently, the court will assess carefully the evidence to decide whether, on the application of normal principles, a finding of beneficial co-ownership can be justified (see *Midland Bank plc* v *Dobson* [1986] 1 FLR 171 at 174 *per* Fox LJ). The relevant principles are mainly derived from the law of trusts but also involve the doctrine of estoppel.

(a) Express trusts
The most straightforward type of case, both for the individuals themselves and also for a mortgagee, is where there is an express declaration of the beneficial entitlement of the owners of the property. This course of action, which has been strongly recommended by the judiciary (see, for example, *Hall* v *Hall* [1984] FLR 126 at 129 *per* Dillon LJ), is most likely to occur when there is legal co-ownership

as well as beneficial co-ownership. In this situation, the only potential problem for a mortgagee, in so far as the question of priorities is concerned, is to ensure that the signatures to the mortgage have not been obtained by improper means (see pp. 57–61).

It is possible, although unusual, for there to be sole legal ownership and equitable co-ownership under an express trust. Any such declaration, to be effective, must be evidenced in writing in order to satisfy the formal requirements of s.53(1)(b) of the Law of Property Act 1925 (see also *Midland Bank plc* v *Dobson* [1986] 1 FLR 171 at 176 *per* Fox LJ). Where a suitably worded declaration of the beneficial interest exists (see *Huntingford* v *Hobbs* (1992) 24 HLR 652 at 655-658), then that declaration is conclusive (see, for example, *Goodman* v *Gallant* (1986)), unless one of the parties can satisfy the rigorous requirements necessary to secure rectification of the trust document (see *Thames Guaranty Ltd* v *Campbell* (1985)). In the absence of any such writing, the claimant to a beneficial interest must establish the interest by relying on a resulting trust, a constructive trust or the principles of equitable estoppel.

(b) Resulting trusts
The typical situation where an argument will be based on the application of the law of resulting and constructive trusts, in the present context, is where a couple have been sharing a property and the legal title to the house is in the sole name of one of them, usually the man, and the other claims, subsequently, to be entitled to a share of the property in equity. Disputes concerning this issue frequently occur on the termination of that relationship and considerable difficulty can then arise in determining whether the woman has any interest in the property at all and then, assuming that she has, ascertaining the quantum of that interest. As this chapter is concerned with the enforcement of rights against a mortgagee, the discussion will focus on the first of these issues.

The task of assessing whether an interest has been acquired in equity has been said to require one to "climb again the familiar ground which slopes down from the twin peaks of *Pettitt* v *Pettitt* (1970) and *Gissing* v *Gissing* (1971)" (*Grant* v *Edwards* [1986] Ch 638 at 646 *per* Nourse LJ).

Pettitt v *Pettitt* concerned a married couple. The house had been conveyed into the sole name of the wife, but the husband claimed to have a beneficial interest in it as a result of decorating work that he had done to it. This claim was unanimously rejected by the House of Lords, on the basis that what had been done was of far too ephemeral a nature to entitle him to an interest in the property. There, nevertheless, followed an extensive review of the law to be applied to this sort of dispute. Although there was a degree of disagreement as to the principles to be applied, the majority view was that, to acquire an interest in the property, the claimant must show entitlement under a resulting trust. This could be done by showing an inferred agreement, at the time that the property was acquired, that there was to be beneficial co-ownership, and for this to be established the claimant must have made a contribution to the purchase of the property.

The emphasis on the application of trust principles to this area of law was reiterated in *Gissing* v *Gissing*. This case again involved a dispute between a husband and wife. In this instance, the house had been conveyed into the sole name of the husband, and the wife claimed to have an interest in it on the basis of having spent some £200 on furnishings and because she had laid a lawn, and bought clothes for herself and their son, and had done "extras" around the house. Her husband paid all the mortgage instalments and had supplied the initial deposit.

In rejecting her claim to an interest in the property, the House of Lords again stressed the need for the claimant to be able to establish an interest under a resulting or constructive trust. To do this it must be possible for the court to infer that there had been an agreement to share the beneficial interest in the home. The court could not impute to the parties an intention that they never had, but might have had if, as reasonable people, they had considered the matter (see [1971] AC 886 at 904 *per* Lord Diplock). For the court to be able to make such an inference, it is necessary for the claimant to have made a significant contribution to the purchase of the house.

Although consistent reference has been made to the need to be able to infer an agreement between the parties as to the beneficial interests that each is to have in the property, this language is a little misleading. If a party has contributed to the purchase of a property, then the assumption is made that there is an intention that a commensurate share is to be acquired in it (see *Gissing* v *Gissing* [1971] AC 886 at 902 *per* Lord Pearson; *Grant* v *Edwards* [1986] Ch 638 at 647 *per* Nourse LJ). This may be so even if the reason why the property was put into one person's name was to further an illegal purpose, such as defrauding the Department of Social Security (*Tinsley* v *Milligan* (1991). Contrast *Tinker* v *Tinker* (1970). See, generally, Jill Martin [1992] Conv 153). It is not necessary to find what interest the parties actually intended that the contributor should acquire; the role of the contribution is both to qualify the contributor to a share in the property and to determine the quantum of it.

In this context, however, the actual intention of the parties is relevant when a party is seeking to establish that there was no intention that an interest was to be acquired. Thus, if it is shown that money was advanced towards the purchase of the property by way of a loan, then the lender will acquire no beneficial interest in the property (*Re Sharpe* (1980)). The onus of proof will be on the person seeking to establish that the payment was in the form of a loan and, if this onus cannot be discharged, a resulting trust will be held to have arisen (*Sekhon* v *Alissa* (1989)). Moreover, even if the money payment was originally made as a loan, a beneficial interest in the property may still be acquired if it transpires that, in the light of subsequent events, it can be seen that the parties ceased to regard the payment in that manner (*Risch* v *McFee* (1991)).

(i) Direct contributions
As has been seen, the prerequisite in order to obtain an interest under a resulting trust is to show that a contribution to the purchase price has been made. The most straightforward type of case is where there are direct cash contributions to the purchase price. Thus in *Re Rogers' Question* (1948), a house was bought for £1,000. The wife contributed £100 and the balance was raised by a loan secured by a mortgage. The husband paid all the mortgage instalments, and the house was conveyed into his name alone. It was held that he held the house on trust, the beneficial interests being in proportion to the size of their contributions: she had a share of one-tenth and he had a share of nine-tenths (see also *Walker* v *Hall* (1983)).

A similar result will occur when the financial contribution is not in the form of the payment of an original lump sum, but instead consists of the payment of mortgage instalments. Although, strictly speaking, no contribution is made to the purchase of the property at the time it is acquired, this is not regarded as a serious objection and it will be held that the contributor has acquired a beneficial interest, commensurate in size to the value of the contribution (*Gissing* v *Gissing* [1971] AC 886 at 906 *per* Lord Diplock. There must be more than the occasional isolated payment: *ibid.* at p. 900 *per* Viscount Dilhorne).

(ii) Indirect contributions
Rather greater difficulty arises when there is no direct payment of part of the purchase price but a person claims a share in the property based upon other contributions to the household, such as looking after the house and bringing up the children. The orthodox view was that such contributions would not give rise to a resulting trust, because they were not referable to the acquisition of the house and, as a result, it was not possible to infer an intention that an interest in the house was to be acquired (see, for example, *Gissing* v *Gissing*; *Savage* v *Dunningham* (1974)).

There developed, nevertheless, a line of authority where a markedly different approach was taken to this situation. This approach was based upon the idea that a constructive trust should be imposed whenever justice and good conscience required it (see *Hussey* v *Palmer* [1972] 1 WLR 1286 at 1289 *per* Lord Denning MR). In determining this question, the view was expressed that reference to contributions to the acquisition of the house should be heard less frequently (*Hazell* v *Hazell* [1972] 1 WLR 301 at 302-304 *per* Lord Denning MR) and that regard should be had to all the circumstances and how much was contributed to the house, not merely in money, but also in keeping up the home and looking after children (*Hall* v *Hall* [1982] 3 FLR 379 at 391 *per* Lord Denning MR).

This approach, which was irreconcilable with earlier authority, has since been repudiated. In *Burns* v *Burns* (1984) an unmarried couple had cohabited for over 17 years. For most of that period, the woman was not in paid employment but looked after the home and their children. She did later secure employment and her earnings were used to meet some of the household expenses and to buy some chattels for the house. It was held in the Court of Appeal that she had acquired no interest in the property. This was because, for her to do so, the court must be able to infer an agreement that she would acquire such an interest; this inference could only be made if she had made a significant contribution to its acquisition – housework and bringing up children were not considered relevant to this issue.

This approach has recently been endorsed in the House of Lords, where it was said that direct contributions to the purchase price by the partner who is not the legal owner, whether initially, or by the payment of mortgage instalments, would readily justify the inference necessary to the creation of a beneficial interest in the home, but it was considered doubtful whether anything less would do (*Lloyds Bank plc* v *Rosset* [1991] AC 107 at 133 *per* Lord Bridge).

This goes a little far, in that it has long been accepted that a beneficial interest in a house can be acquired by indirect contributions to its purchase. Such contributions must, however, be substantial in nature and also referable to the purchase of the property. The type of indirect contribution that will suffice is when the claimant uses her earnings to meet the household expenses, thereby enabling her partner to use his resources to pay the mortgage instalments (see *Gissing* v *Gissing* [1971] AC 886 at 908 *per* Lord Diplock). Again, if the person claiming an interest in the property works in the family business, the profits of which are used to finance the purchase of the house, this will suffice (see, for example, *Re Cummins* (1972); *Bothe* v *Amos* (1976)). Nevertheless, it is now abundantly clear that, to acquire an interest in a house under a resulting trust, conduct of a purchasing nature will be essential – and that contributions to the household of a general or a domestic nature will be insufficient.

(c) Constructive trusts

As has been seen, the basis of the resulting trust is that one infers an intention to share the beneficial interest in the property from the fact that both parties have contributed to its acquisition, although the legal title may have been conveyed into the name of only one of them. The size of the beneficial share of each party is then determined by the size of their respective contributions. There also exists, however, a line of cases where there is no need to seek to establish, *by inference*, what the parties agreed as to the beneficial ownership of the property – rather, there is evidence of an *actual* agreement with regard to this matter. In such cases, the constructive trust has an important role to play.

(i) Contribution

If the legal title has been conveyed to one person, P, but it is agreed that another person, Q, should have a beneficial interest in it, then, unless that agreement is evidenced in writing, it is ineffectual to confer upon Q a beneficial interest because the requirements of s.53(1)(b) of the Law of Property Act 1925 have not been complied with (see also p. 38). However, where Q, in reliance upon the agreement, has contributed to the purchase price, then it becomes inequitable for P to rely on the lack of written evidence of the declaration of trust and claim to be solely entitled to the property both at law and in equity. To do so would be to use a statute as an instrument of fraud and, to prevent this, a constructive trust will be imposed to enforce the original agreement (see *Rochefoucauld* v *Bousted* (1897); *Bannister* v *Bannister* (1948)).

Although this principle did not originate in the context of co-ownership of the home, it has been applied to these circumstances in a number of cases. In *Eves* v *Eves* (1975) a couple moved into a house together. The house was conveyed into his name alone, he having told her that her name could not go on to the title deeds because she was under 21 years of age. It was nevertheless understood, at least by her, on the basis of what she had been told, that she was to have a share in the property. The house was in a dilapidated condition, and she did a considerable amount of work to it, including wielding a 14 lb sledge-hammer. Enforcing what was taken to be the prior agreement, the court held that she was entitled to a one-quarter beneficial share in the house, under a constructive trust.

This decision was approved and applied in *Grant* v *Edwards* (1986). In this case, a couple were moving into a house. It was conveyed into his name alone, the reason being that to put it into their joint names was regarded as unwise in that it might affect any order made in divorce proceedings that were pending between her and her then husband. The whole of the deposit was supplied by him, and he also paid the mortgage instalments. She did, however, make a significant contribution to the household expenditure – without her contribution he could not have continued to service the mortgage repayments. On the breakdown of their relationship, the issue arose as to the beneficial ownership of the house and it was held, applying the principle of *Eves* v *Eves*, that she was entitled to a half share in equity under a constructive trust (see also *Stokes* v *Anderson* (1991); *Hammond* v *Mitchell* (1991)).

The basis of the decision, which has subsequently been approved in the House of Lords (*Lloyds Bank plc* v *Rosset* (1991)), was not that the extent of her contribution was such that it entitled her to a half share in the property. Rather, the fact that there had been a pretext for not putting the legal title to the house in their joint names gave rise to the necessary implication that it was understood between them that the house was to be jointly owned beneficially. Accordingly, a constructive trust was imposed to give effect to the presumed agreement.

(ii) Agreement

The most distinctive difference between the resulting trust and the constructive trust is that the former operates to give the claimant a beneficial share which corresponds in amount to the value of the contribution, that being the presumed intention of the parties, whereas the constructive trust operates to enforce the actual agreement that the parties have made, irrespective of the value of the contribution.

This distinction is, perhaps, most clearly illustrated in *Re Densham* (1975). A house was conveyed to a husband who was registered as sole proprietor. Subsequently he was declared bankrupt and a principal issue in the case was how much of the equity in the house should be available to the trustee in bankruptcy. It was found as a fact that the couple regarded themselves as joint and equal owners of their property, this agreement extending to the house. In terms of her financial contribution to the purchase of it, however, the wife had contributed approximately one-ninth. Hence it was found that, under a constructive trust imposed to give effect to the actual agreement, she was entitled to a half share in the property, whereas, if her entitlement had been under a resulting trust, she would have been entitled to only a one-ninth share in it. This was important, because Goff J also held that the difference between a half and one-ninth was a voluntary settlement which could be set aside under s.42 of the Bankruptcy Act 1914 (now the Insolvency Act 1986, s.334).

The constructive trust, therefore, when imposed, will give effect to an actual antecedent agreement as to the beneficial entitlement (see also *Lloyds Bank plc* v *Rosset* [1991] AC 107 at 132-133 *per* Lord Bridge). Normally this will amount to a half share, because it is not usually the case that a couple, when about to buy a house together, agree to share the property in different proportions – although this is, of course, possible as, for example, where what is agreed upon is a life interest in the property (see *Ungurian* v *Lesnoff* (1990)).

In addition to there being an agreement to share the beneficial ownership of the home, the claimant must also make a contribution to its acquisition. This requirement seems to be treated rather more liberally than is the case when resulting trusts are involved. In the case of resulting trusts, the claimant must show a contribution that is referable to the acquisition of the house. Where constructive trusts are concerned, it does not seem to be necessary to show a direct link between the agreement and the acquisition of the house. Although the basis of the constructive trust, in the present context, was to prevent the unjust enrichment of the owner of the legal title, the courts seem to have extended the notion of what will amount to a sufficient contribution to include conduct upon which the claimant would not have embarked unless there had been an agreement that she was to have some interest in the house. Such conduct can undoubtedly be the incurring of expenditure which is referable to the acquisition of the house, but it need not necessarily be so (*Grant* v *Edwards* [1986] Ch 638 at 647 *per* Nourse LJ; *Lloyds Bank plc* v *Rosset* [1991] AC 107 at 129 *per* Lord Bridge). The principles underlying the constructive trust bear a close similarity to those underlying equitable estoppel, with which parallels have been drawn (*Grant* v *Edwards* at p. 656 *per* Sir Nicolas Browne-Wilkinson V-C; *Lloyds Bank plc* v *Rosset* at p. 129 *per* Lord Bridge) and to which attention must now be turned.

(d) Equitable estoppel
The doctrine of equitable or proprietary estoppel is an ancient one (see, for example, *Hunt* v *Carew* (1649)). The essence of the doctrine is that where one person, A, has acted to his detriment on the faith of a belief, which was known to and encouraged by another person, B, that he either has or is going to be given a right in or over B's property, B cannot insist upon his strict legal rights if to do so would be inconsistent with A's belief (*Re Basham* [1986] 1 WLR 1498 at 1503 *per* Mr Edward Nugee QC).

The doctrine of equitable estoppel has been applied to a number of informal transactions affecting land. For example, in *Inwards* v *Baker* (1965), a father encouraged his son to extend his bungalow on to land owned by the father. On the death of the father, an attempt was made to evict the son. The action failed. The father having encouraged his son to believe that he would have rights over his land, and the son having relied on that belief, an estoppel right was created. This right was satisfied by declaring that the son had an indefinite right to occupy the land and that this was binding upon the father's successor in title.

A number of features should be noted about this decision. First, it was immaterial that the precise nature of the son's expectation was undefined. It was sufficient to show that the son had *some* expectation of acquiring rights over his father's land. The reason for this is that, when a court is dealing with a case of equitable estoppel, there is considerable discretion as to how to satisfy the equitable right that has arisen. Equity is seen here at its most flexible (*Crabb* v *Arun D.C.* [1976] Ch 179 at 189 *per* Lord Denning MR), and does not require the same degree of certainty as is necessary to establish a contract. Second, the case also illustrates that the rights which arise from estoppel are potentially binding on third parties; a factor which may have repercussions for mortgagees.

(i) Raising the estoppel
It was formerly the case that, to establish the existence of rights arising from estoppel, various criteria had to be established. These crite-

ria, known as the five *probanda* (see *Willmott* v *Barber* (1880) 15 Ch D 96 at 105-106 *per* Fry J), were based essentially on the notion of mistake as to legal rights, and, although oft-cited, they were not appropriate to a number of situations where estoppel was in issue. Accordingly, although these criteria have occasionally resurfaced in modern case law (see *Coombes* v *Smith* (1986)), the modern tendency is to view the doctrine as a flexible one, untrammelled by excessive formality.

In *Taylors Fashions Ltd* v *Liverpool Victoria Trustees Co Ltd* (1981), Oliver J analysed the development of equitable estoppel and concluded that the underlying principle was that of unconscionability; the central issue in each case being whether it is unconscionable for one party to deny that which, knowingly or unknowingly, he has allowed or encouraged the other to act upon to his detriment.

This analysis, which has secured subsequent judicial endorsement (see, for example, *Habib Bank Ltd* v *Habib Bank AG Zurich* [1981] 1 WLR 1265 at 1285; *A-G of Hong Kong* v *Humphreys Estate (Queen's Gardens) Ltd* [1987] AC 114 at 121. But contrast *Coombes* v *Smith* (1986)), requires the court to undertake a detailed examination of the facts to determine this essential criterion of unconscionability. In the present context, what must be shown is that the claimant had some expectation of having some interest, however ill-defined, in her partner's property. In reliance thereon, there must have been some conduct, the result of which is that it is unconscionable for her partner to deny her some remedy.

A good example of such a case is *Maharaj* v *Chand* (1986). The defendant, who was living in secure rented accommodation of her own, formed an attachment with the plaintiff. On securing his assurance that she would always have a roof over her head, she left her own property and moved into his flat. She also made contributions from her earnings to the household expenditure and looked after the family. On the breakdown of the relationship, the plaintiff sought possession. The Privy Council held that she was entitled to remain in the property indefinitely. She had the clear expectation of secure accommodation and had relied upon that expectation. As a result, an equity arose in her favour, which was satisfied by giving her a personal and indefinite right of occupancy.

In contrast to this case, reference should also be made to the unsatisfactory decision in *Coombes* v *Smith* (1986). In this unusual case, the defendant was unhappily married when she met the plaintiff, who was also married. He acquired a house into which she moved, leaving her husband in the matrimonial home. She made no direct financial contribution to the acquisition of the house but did redecorate it and also carried out some improvements to it. She looked after their child and also decided not to look for employment, in order that she could continue to stay at home to look after the child. On the breakdown of the relationship, the issue arose as to whether she was entitled under the doctrine of estoppel to any rights in the house.

The judge held that she was not. The main reason for this was that he concluded that she was unable to establish that she had acted in reliance on any expectation of acquiring an interest in the property. Instead, the view was taken that all of her claimed acts of reliance were explicable on the basis that they were an inherent part of her relationship with the plaintiff. This, with respect, seems rather a harsh view. Although the decision can be reconciled with that in *Maharaj* v *Chand*, the two decisions do not sit easily together in terms of their approaches to this type of situation. It remains to be seen whether the courts are prepared to adopt a more liberal line when dealing with this type of case. An argument based upon estoppel will be stronger, however, if the woman can point to such factors as her giving up employment (see, for example, *Jones (A.E.)* v *Jones (F.W.)* (1977)) or her own secure accommodation in reliance upon her obtaining security in the property into which she is moving, or has moved.

(ii) Satisfying the estoppel

Very much a distinguishing feature of equitable estoppel is its flexibility. Once it has been held that an equity has arisen, the manner in which it is then satisfied is a matter of discretion: "equity is seen here at its most flexible" (*Crabb* v *Arun D.C.* [1976] Ch 179 at 189 *per* Lord Denning MR). Because of this element of discretion, cases can only serve as illustrations of how the courts may act; some principles have, however, emerged.

The starting point is to ascertain the full nature of the expectation, the satisfaction of this being the limit of the remedy that can be granted (see *Dodsworth* v *Dodsworth* (1973)). Thus in one case, a man had promised his partner that he would give her the house and its contents. She relied upon this by expending money on improvements to the house. To satisfy the equity that had arisen, he was ordered to convey the house to her: *Pascoe* v *Turner* (1979).

From the fact that in this case the court ordered that the expectation be satisfied in full, it should not be thought that this will be the necessary result in all cases. The court will have regard to all the circumstances of the case and seek to achieve a remedy that will meet the justice of the case. A principal object that the courts seek to achieve is to ensure secure accommodation for the person in whose favour the estoppel has arisen. To achieve this, an indefinite right to remain in the property may be given (see *Inwards* v *Baker* (1965); *Maharaj* v *Chand* (1986)), or the lesser right to remain in occupation until compensation has been made for any expenditure incurred in reliance on the expectation (see *Dodsworth* v *Dodsworth* (1973); *Re Sharpe* (1980)). A further possibility is that the court may order the grant of a long lease that is not assignable (see *Griffiths* v *Williams* (1977)).

Given the wide discretion that exists, one cannot be too dogmatic in predicting the results of cases. Where the relationship between the parties is akin to that of marriage, however, the courts are likely to be influenced by family law considerations in the exercise of their discretion, with the result that the existence of children may be an important criterion for the court. As the courts have also stressed recently the close affinity between estoppel and the constructive trust, it can be expected that, in some cases, the equity will be satisfied by declaring that the woman is entitled to a beneficial share in the house.

Equitable estoppel may well have serious consequences for a mortgagee who is seeking possession – the question of the enforcement of equitable third party rights against mortgagees must now be considered.

2. Co-owners and mortgagees: the priority of rights

Once it has been established that beneficial co-ownership exists, it is necessary to ascertain the circumstances in which such rights will be binding on the mortgagee.

(a) Registered land
The starting point in a discussion of this area is the decision of the House of Lords in *Williams & Glyn's Bank Ltd* v *Boland* (1980). Title to the house was registered in the sole name of Mr Boland but it was conceded that Mrs Boland was beneficial co-owner of it. He subsequently mortgaged the house to the bank, which made no enquiries of Mrs Boland, who was living there at all material times. After Mr Boland had defaulted on the mortgage, the bank sought possession and the issue was whether Mrs Boland's interest took effect as an overriding interest and was, therefore, binding on the bank.

In deciding against the bank, the House of Lords held that Mrs Boland's interest as a beneficial tenant in common, although a minor interest, became an overriding interest within s.70(1)(g) of the Land Registration Act 1925 if she was also in actual occupation of the property. In holding her to be in actual occupation, the court considered that the argument to the contrary, that her occupation was to be regarded as a shadow of her husband's, was "heavily obsolete". Instead, the issue of whether a person was in actual occupation was regarded as being one of fact and, in determining this issue, analogies with the concept of notice were not considered to be relevant (see [1981] AC 487 at 504 *per* Lord Wilberforce).

(i) Actual occupation
It was made clear in *Boland* that the question of whether a person is in actual occupation is one of fact. Nevertheless, some guidance can be obtained from the case law as to what will constitute actual occupation. For a person to be in actual occupation, there must be some degree of permanence and continuity – this rules out a mere fleeting presence (see *Abbey National Building Society* v *Cann* [1991] AC 56 at 93 *per* Lord Oliver). Thus, a person who is allowed access

to a property, in order to plan decoration or measure up for furnishings, will not be regarded as being in actual occupation. Neither will the sporadic parking of a car on the property be sufficient (*Epps* v *Esso Petroleum Ltd* (1973), although contrast *Kling* v *Keston Properties Ltd* (1984)).

Although some degree of permanence is necessary, there is no requirement that the occupation be continuous for actual occupation to be established. For example, if a person stays at a property for a few days each week, it is likely that she will be held to be in actual occupation (cf *Kingsnorth Finance Co Ltd* v *Tizard* (1986)). Similarly, absence from the property for a period will not necessarily prevent actual occupation from being established. In *Chhokar* v *Chhokar* (1984), a husband conveyed the matrimonial home to an associate while his wife, who was a beneficial co-owner, was in hospital having their child. Not surprisingly, she was held to be in actual occupation and therefore able to establish an overriding interest binding upon the purchaser. Where the absence from the property is more prolonged, however, perhaps due to reasons of employment, or a prolonged illness, then it is thought that the lengthier the absence, the greater the visible sign of an intention to return will be necessary in order to establish actual occupation. This is likely to mean the leaving of personal effects in the property.

(ii) The time of occupation
An important issue in this context is to determine the relevant time at which actual occupation must be established. There are two possibilities. These are (i) the date when the transaction takes place, or (ii) the date when registration is effected. Because the latter date is when the legal title passes to the purchaser and to the mortgagee (see LRA 1925, ss.19(1), 20(1), 26(1)), principle would seem to indicate that this should be the time when actual occupation would be relevant. Because there is a time lag between the completion of the transaction and the application for registration, this view led to the practical difficulty that a person could go into occupation between the completion of the transaction and the application for its registration. A mortgagee could, therefore, be bound by an overriding interest which came into being between the execution of the mortgage

deed and the application for its registration. To avoid this possibility, the House of Lords held in *Abbey National Building Society* v *Cann* that the earlier of the two dates is the one by which the person asserting the overriding interest must be in actual occupation.

(b) Unregistered land

Where title to the land is unregistered, the question of whether a mortgagee is bound by the rights of a beneficial tenant in common is not answered by simply asking if that person is in actual occupation of the property. The test is whether the mortgagee, as a purchaser of a legal estate, could have discovered the existence of the equitable interest by making reasonable enquiries (LPA 1925, s.199).

At one time it was accepted that, if the mortgagor was in occupation of the house, enquiries need not be addressed to other occupiers of the property (*Caunce* v *Caunce* (1969)). Such a view no longer represents the law and it is clear, after the decision in *Boland*, that for enquiries to be reasonable they must be made of all the occupiers of the property, regardless of whether the mortgagor is also in occupation (see *Midland Bank Ltd* v *Farmpride Hatcheries Ltd* (1980)). Nevertheless, there may be situations when the result of a case may depend upon whether or not title is registered.

Although it was accepted in *Kingsnorth Finance Co* v *Tizard* [1986] 1 WLR 783 at 794-795 that an inspection of the property at a time pre-arranged with the mortgagor did not exhaust the ambit of reasonable enquiries, this seems to go too far (see MP Thompson [1986] Conv 283). In any event, it is possible to envisage situations, such as where the co-owner is away in hospital, when reasonable enquiries would not discover her existence but, if title to the land were registered, she would be held to be in actual occupation and thus have an overriding interest. In such circumstances, the result of a case would differ according to whether or not title were registered. Such cases are likely to be few. In most cases, it will make no difference whether title is registered or unregistered. As all land is now within an area of compulsory registration of title (see Registration of Title Order 1989 (S.I. 1989 No. 1347)), the importance of this possible disparity will steadily decline.

3. Limitations on Boland

(a) First mortgages
The decision in *Boland* generated considerable concern; so much so, that the matter was referred to the Law Commission, which recommended that the decision should be reversed by legislation, so that a person in the position of Mrs Boland could only enforce her rights against a mortgagee if they were protected in the appropriate manner by registration (see (1982) Law Com. No. 115). In fact, no legislation has ensued, and the matter has been left to case law. As will be seen, most, if not all, of the concern generated by *Boland* has been assuaged by later decisions.

In the immediate aftermath of *Boland*, a great deal of concern was felt by building societies about the enforceability of their securities. The perceived problem was when a house was being bought with the aid of a mortgage and was being conveyed into the name of one person, H, but another person, W, was also going to move into the property and contribute to the purchase of it. In that situation, W would acquire a beneficial interest in the house and that interest, it was feared, would bind the mortgagee. The lending institutions adopted quite elaborate precautions to protect themselves from this danger but, in the light of recent decisions, it has emerged that the danger is more apparent than real.

In *Bristol & West Building Society* v *Henning* (1985), a house was purchased for £12,900, of which £11,000 was secured by a mortgage. The house was conveyed into Mr Henning's name alone, but it was established that Mrs Henning was entitled to a beneficial half share of the property in equity. When Mr Henning defaulted on the mortgage, the plaintiff sought possession and Mrs Henning argued that her interest was binding on the society. Rejecting her argument, the Court of Appeal held, because she knew that the mortgage was being executed and, indeed, that the house could not have been purchased without it, that the intention should be imputed to her that the mortgagee should have priority over her. This was so, despite her not having given any thought to this issue.

Although the reasoning has been criticised on the basis that the authorities establish that the court should seek to infer what the parties intended rather than imputing to them intentions that they would have formed had they considered the matter (see MP Thompson (1986) 49 MLR 245; Jill Martin (1986) 16 Fam Law 315), the result seems sensible. It is difficult to see why a woman in the position of Mrs Henning, who has benefited considerably from the mortgage, should subsequently be able to assert that her interest has priority over that of the mortgagee. More importantly, the decision has been followed in *Paddington Building Society* v *Mendelsohn* (1985) and enjoys the tacit support of the House of Lords (*Abbey National Building Society* v *Cann* (1990)).

The effect of the decision in *Henning* is important. It means that when the purchase of a house is, in part, financed by a mortgage, then it will be virtually impossible for the rights of beneficial co-owners to gain priority over those of a mortgagee. The number of instances when W does not know that a mortgage is being obtained to finance the purchase of the property must inevitably be extremely few (for a rare example, see *Lloyds Bank plc* v *Rosset* (1990)). Moreover, even if that rare event does occur, it will be difficult for W to establish that she was in actual occupation before the mortgage took effect, that event now legally, as well as factually, being contemporaneous with the conveyance or transfer (*Abbey National Building Society* v *Cann* (1990)). It therefore follows that a mortgagee who is lending money to finance the purchase of a property can regard the *Boland* decision with equanimity.

The reasoning employed in *Henning* has recently been extended. In *Equity and Law Home Loans Ltd* v *Prestidge* (1991), a house was conveyed into the sole name of Mr Prestidge but his partner, a Mrs Brown, was a beneficial co-owner of it. The house was subject to a mortgage of £30,000 in favour of the Britannia Building Society, that mortgage having been taken out to finance the purchase of the house. Subsequently, Mr Prestidge approached Equity and Law with a view to re-mortgaging the property. They were informed of Mrs Brown's interest in the property but were content to rely upon Mr Prestidge to obtain her consent to the transaction. He then borrowed by way of mortgage over £42,000. He used £30,000 to discharge the mortgage in favour of Britannia and pocketed the remainder. The issues in the ensuing litigation were whether Equity and Law were entitled to possession of the property as against Mrs Brown and, if so, what was to happen to the proceeds of sale after the property had been sold. It was held that the mortgagee was entitled to possession but only had priority over Mrs Brown in respect of the first £30,000 of the loan.

It was conceded, on the basis of *Henning*, that Britannia would, as against Mrs Brown, have been entitled to possession. From this, it was further reasoned that, if another mortgage had been created to replace that one, perhaps because the repayment terms were more favourable, then the subsequent mortgagee should be in the same position as Britannia. It was therefore decided that Equity and Law should be treated as if they had simply replaced Britannia and, in consequence, they had priority over Mrs Brown to the limited extent described above.

It is submitted that this reasoning is questionable (see, further, MP Thompson [1992] Conv 206). The result of the case is effectively to subrogate Equity and Law to the position of Britannia. This, however, is not an automatic process. Ordinarily for subrogation to take place, it is necessary for the purpose of the loan to be to pay off the earlier security (see *Orakpo* v *Manson Investments Ltd* [1978] AC 95 at 105 *per* Lord Diplock). This was not the case in *Prestidge* and, it is submitted, Equity and Law should not have been held to have had the limited degree of priority accorded to them.

(b) Legal co-ownership

An important fact in *Boland* was that the legal title was vested in only one person. The issue that subsequently arose was whether the result would have been different had the mortgage been executed by two trustees for sale. In *City of London Building Society* v *Flegg* (1987) a property, appropriately called Bleak House, was transferred to a Mr and Mrs Maxwell-Brown. It was common ground, however, that the Maxwell-Browns held the property on trust for themselves and the Fleggs, who were the parents of Mrs Maxwell-Brown. Part of the finance for the house purchase was supplied by the Abbey National Building Society, and it was conceded that that mortgage would have had priority over the interest of the Fleggs. Subsequently, and without consulting the Fleggs, the Maxwell-

Browns re-mortgaged the property on several other occasions until, finally, the house was mortgaged to the plaintiffs and the money borrowed was used to discharge all the existing mortgages. When the Maxwell-Browns defaulted on the mortgage, the plaintiffs sought possession. The Fleggs, who had been in actual occupation of the property at all material times, argued that they had an overriding interest binding upon the plaintiffs.

This argument failed. The House of Lords distinguished *Boland* on the basis that in *Boland* the mortgage had been executed by only one legal co-owner of the property. The existence of beneficial co-ownership gave rise to an implied trust for sale (see *Bull* v *Bull* (1955)) and, in such circumstances, one trustee for sale could not overreach the beneficial interests existing behind the trust. In *Flegg*, however, there were two trustees for sale who consequently were able to overreach the interests existing behind the trust. It was immaterial whether there were four or forty-four people entitled behind the trust for sale. Because the mortgage was executed by two trustees, the beneficial interests of the beneficiaries were overreached and took effect only against the equity of redemption.

The decision in *Flegg,* which, interestingly, and in contrast with its reaction to the decision in *Boland,* the Law Commission has recommended be reversed by legislation – in order that the rights of people in actual occupation of land should be fully protected ((1989) Law Com. No. 188) – clearly establishes that, if the mortgagee deals with at least two legal owners, then there is no need to worry about the rights of beneficial co-owners. Their interests will be overreached. However, potential problems still remain where there is forgery or where the consent of a co-owner to the mortgage is liable to be disregarded owing to the presence of some vitiating factor.

(i) Forgery

A problem may arise when the legal title to the house is in joint names, H and W, and the property is mortgaged, H having forged W's signature. This occurred in *First National Securities Ltd* v *Hegerty* (1984). In that case, H and W were beneficial joint tenants. It was held that the effect of the forgery was to sever the beneficial joint tenancy, and the mortgage then operated as a charge over H's beneficial share. In default, the mortgagee can then bring proceedings under the Charging Orders Act 1979. If, after such a forgery occurs, the mortgage is registered, then the innocent co-owner will be able to obtain rectification of the register (see *Norwich and Peterborough Building Society* v *Steed* [1992] 3 WLR 669 at 682 *per* Scott LJ).

(ii) Vitiating factors to consents
As has been seen, where a mortgage has been created for the purpose of financing the purchase of a house, it will be almost impossible for a co-owner to establish that her beneficial interest is binding upon the mortgagee. Where the mortgage is not created for this purpose, however, then unless advantage can be taken of the *Prestidge* decision, the mortgagee may face very real difficulties in ensuring that the mortgage has priority over any competing interests.

Difficulties can arise in two related situations:
(i) if the house is in the name of one person, H, the mortgagee must take steps to ensure that other people do not have beneficial interests in it which will be binding upon the mortgagee;
(ii) if the house is in the joint names of H and W, and H wishes to borrow by way of mortgage for his own purposes, then considerable care must be taken in obtaining from W the requisite signature to the mortgage, if the mortgage is not, as against her, liable subsequently to be set aside. This will be true, also, if the consent to the mortgage of an occupying co-owner needs to be obtained.

The first of these problems has already been considered (see pp. 50 – 52). This section is concerned with the second of these difficulties. The main problem to be considered is the nature of the precautions that the mortgagee must take if the validity of the mortgage, as against W, is not to be impeached.

Agency: Until recently, it was thought that the validity of a mortgage could be challenged on one of two grounds. The first was where the mortgagee had entrusted the borrower with the task of obtaining the signature of the other co-owner. In these circumstances, the courts would regard the borrower as the agent of the mortgagee, so that if undue influence was used to obtain the signature, or if the nature of the transaction was misrepresented, then this misconduct would be attributed to the mortgagee, with the result that the mortgage would not be binding as against W.

A good example of this type of case is provided by *Kings North Trust Ltd* v *Bell* (1986) (see also *Turnbull & Co* v *Duval* (1902); *Avon Finance Co Ltd* v *Bridger* (1979)). In this case, a mortgage was created over the matrimonial home, the wife's signature to it having been obtained after its nature had been misrepresented to her by her husband. In deciding whether the mortgage should be set aside, it was said that "... the key question in the present case is whether ... the plaintiffs are to be treated as having left it to the [husband] to procure the execution of their mortgage ... by the [wife] with the result that the plaintiffs are answerable for the fraudulent misrepresentation made to [her] to achieve that end" ([1986] 1 WLR 119 at 124 *per* Dillon LJ).

Having decided that was indeed the case, it was held that the mortgage should be set aside as against the wife.

Undue influence: The other basis upon which a mortgage is vulnerable to being set aside is where the mortgagee uses undue influence to procure W's signature or, far more likely, has notice that undue influence was used. A good example of the latter occurred in *Bank of Credit and Commerce International SA* v *Aboody* (1989). In this case, H was not entrusted with the task of obtaining W's signature. Instead, W was asked to sign in the office of a solicitor, who was acting for the bank. While the matter was being discussed, H stormed into the room and a shouting match developed, after which W signed the mortgage. She subsequently argued that it should be set aside as against her.

It was made clear that the court could set aside the transaction on one of two grounds: agency or undue influence (see [1990] 1 QB 923 at 972-973 *per* Slade LJ). In this case, it was accepted that the argument must be based on the latter ground. To establish this, various criteria were enumerated. These were:
(i) the other party to the transaction (or someone who induced the transaction for his own benefit) had the capacity to influence

the complainant;
(ii) the influence was exercised;
(iii) its exercise was undue;
(iv) the undue influence brought the transaction about;
(v) the transaction was manifestly disadvantageous to the complainant.

On the facts of the case the first four criteria were satisfied, in that the bank had notice of the use of undue influence. W's argument failed because she could not prove that the transaction was to her manifest disadvantage (but contrast *Barclays Bank plc* v *Kennedy* (1989)).

A wider principle: As this area of the law developed, it was generally thought that a mortgage would be set aside at W's instigation if, and only if, H had been allowed to act as the mortgagor's agent and he was guilty of undue influence or misrepresentation, or the mortgagee had notice of the use of undue influence. Thus, in a number of cases where the transaction had not been fully understood, the mortgage was nevertheless upheld as these criteria had not been satisfied (see *Coldunell Ltd* v *Gallon* (1986); *Lloyds Bank plc* v *Egremont* (1990)). If, however, the mortgagee had purported to explain the transaction, liability in negligence could ensue if the explanation was inadequate: *Midland Bank plc* v *Perry* (1988). In the recent case of *Barclays Bank plc* v *O'Brien* (1992), however, the Court of Appeal asserted that a wider principle existed.

In this case, H acted as guarantor for the overdraft of a company with which he was closely associated. The bank sought security over the matrimonial home, which was in the joint names of him and his wife, W. Although instructions were issued within the bank that the mortgage be fully explained to W, the clerk who dealt with the matter did not do this. Instead, W came into a branch of the bank and signed the mortgage deed without having first read it. She thought that the mortgage was to secure the existing overdraft, which at that time was £64,000, whereas in fact the mortgage secured all monies. When the bank sought to enforce its security the level of indebtedness was considerably in excess of this sum. It was held, despite it being found that the bank had not used H as its agent, and that it had

had no notice of any undue influence exerted by H upon W, that, as against W, the mortgage was only enforceable to secure the sum of £64,000.

In reaching this conclusion, the Court of Appeal held that the earlier authorities rested on a general principle of equity that, where a husband entered into a transaction for his benefit, then the mortgagee must ensure that the wife fully understands the true nature of the transaction. This principle extends also to relationships other than husband and wife, to include any relationship where the borrower is likely to be able to exert influence over the other party – for example, a child or elderly parents. In the present case, the bank had not ensured that W fully understood the mortgage, and so it was only enforceable against her to a limited extent.

Coping with the new principle: The decision in *O'Brien* must be seen as highly controversial, in that the authorities relied upon seem to provide little, if any, support for such a wide principle, and some authorities are opposed to it (see MP Thompson [1992] Conv 443). Pending any review of it, however, consideration must be given to how to come to terms with it.

From the point of view of lenders, the decision should not occasion too much alarm. If they write separately to W, counselling that she take independent legal advice before executing the document, it seems that the mortgage will not be set aside even if that advice is not heeded: *Coldunell Ltd* v *Gallon* (1986). Indeed, it is common practice to entrust the obtaining of W's signature to a solicitor, who will certify that he has explained the document to her. The difficulty is likely to be felt by the solicitor.

It is likely that the solicitor that W sees is the one employed by H. In such a situation, the solicitor faces a potential conflict of interests. His client, H, needs to obtain W's signature. The mortgage may not, however, be in W's interest, and thus the solicitor should advise her not to sign. His failure to do so may well give rise to liability to her in negligence. If, however, he does advise her not to sign, then it would appear that he is in breach of his duty to H. Because of this, it seems that the same solicitor should not act for H and W in a transaction of this type. This may cause practical problems when he recommends that W should instruct a different firm of solicitors with the additional cost to the family budget that this will entail.

In conclusion, it may be said that the rights of co-owners are a potential problem area for mortgagees. These problems do not affect mortgagees who are lending money to enable a house to be purchased, but will cause considerable difficulty to mortgagees lending for other purposes.

Chapter 3

The sale of mortgaged property

A. The power of sale

For the mortgagee to be able to sell the mortgaged property, the statutory requirements regulating the power of sale must be satisfied. The relevant provisions are contained in ss.101 and 103 of the Law of Property Act 1925 – s.101 is concerned with when the power of sale arises, and s.103 with when it becomes exercisable. These provisions will be dealt with in turn.

1. The power arising

Section 101 provides that:
>A mortgagee, where the mortgage is made by deed, shall by virtue of this Act, have the following powers ...
>(i) A power, when the mortgage money has become due, to sell, or to concur with any other person in selling, either subject to prior charges or not, and either together or in lots, by public auction or by private contract, subject to such conditions respecting title, or evidence of title, or other matter, as the mortgagee thinks fit, with power to vary any contract for sale, and to buy in at an auction, or to rescind any contract for sale,

and to re-sell, without being answerable for any loss occasioned thereby ....

The following various points should be noted about this provision.

(a) Deed
For the statutory power of sale to arise, it is necessary for the mortgage to be made by deed. In the case of legal mortgages, this obviously presents no problem as all legal mortgages must be created by deed. An equitable mortgage does not have to be created by deed, however, and to ensure that the power of sale can arise, it is common to execute a deed when such a mortgage is created. If this course is not adopted, the mortgagee can bring a foreclosure action, and the court is then empowered under s.91(2) of the Law of Property Act 1925 to order a sale. (See *Oldham v Stringer* (1884).)

(b) Purchase money due
It is in order to satisfy this provision that it is common to find in mortgage agreements a clause to the effect that the whole sum borrowed is to be repaid within a short period, traditionally six months, after the creation of the mortgage. This scheme is artificial, but the artificiality can be avoided by the use of a default clause, whereby the whole capital sum becomes payable upon the mortgagor's failing to meet his repayment obligations. It has been pointed out (H Potter (1932) 48 LQR 158 at 159) that there is a potential difficulty, inherent in this method, of proving to a purchaser that there has been a default: a matter of considerable importance in establishing that the mortgagee has the power of sale. This difficulty can be overcome by the inclusion of a clause, whereby the mortgage money becomes payable upon demand (see *Bank of Baroda v Panessar* (1986)).

Where the mortgage contains neither a default clause nor a provision for the whole sum to be repaid at a specified time soon after the mortgage was created, the requirement that the purchase money is due can cause difficulty. In the case of instalment mortgages, the mortgagee's position is usually satisfactory. In *Payne v Cardiff RDC* (1932) the money borrowed was repayable in instalments. On default by the mortgagor, it was held that the purchase money was due, within the meaning of the Act, despite the whole sum's not being payable at that time.

Logically, it should follow from this decision that the purchase money should be regarded as being due from the date of the first instalment, regardless of default. In subsequent decisions, however, it has been held that, in the case of instalment mortgages, the power of sale does not arise until there has been default in repayments: *De Borman v Makkofaides* (1971); *Twentieth Century Banking Corporation Ltd v Wilkinson* (1976). In both these cases, however, the mortgage deeds were poorly drafted and had the effect of excluding the power of sale, except in certain events, so that the general position is not entirely clear. In the case of an endowment mortgage, the capital sum is not payable until the end of the agreed term, so that it is important for the mortgagee to include a clause in the mortgage deed enabling the power of sale to arise at an earlier date. A failure to do so will necessitate the bringing of foreclosure proceedings and an order for a sale in lieu. For it to be possible to adopt this course, however, it is necessary that the mortgagor should be in breach of some obligation imposed by the mortgage, the adherence to which is a necessary element in keeping the mortgagor's right to redeem alive (see *Twentieth Century Banking Corporation Ltd v Wilkinson* [1977] Ch 99 at 104 *per* Templeman J).

(c) Power not arising

It is critical, from the perspective of the purchaser, to ensure that the power of sale has arisen. Provided that the power of sale has arisen, the mortgagee can, under s.104(1) of the Law of Property Act 1925, convey the property free from all estates over which he has priority: i.e. the mortgagor's equity of redemption is overreached. If the power of sale has not arisen, however, then he does not have this power and all that he can convey is his own interest in the property, i.e. the mortgage. The purchaser must always ensure, therefore, that the mortgagee's power of sale has arisen.

THE SALE OF MORTGAGED PROPERTY

2. The power becoming exercisable

Once the power of sale has arisen, it becomes exercisable if any of the following conditions laid down by s.103 of the Law of Property Act 1925 are satisfied. These are that:
(i) Notice requiring payment of the mortgage money has been served on the mortgagor or one of two or more mortgagors, and default has been made in payment of the mortgage money, or part thereof for three months after such service; or
(ii) Some interest under the mortgage is in arrear and unpaid for two months after becoming due; or
(iii) There has been a breach of some provision contained in the mortgage deed or in this Act ... on the part of the mortgagor ... to be observed or performed, other than and besides a covenant for payment of the mortgage money or interest thereon.

As is the case with the conditions laid down by s.101, the requirements of s.103 can be varied by the mortgage deed (see LPA 1925, s.101(3)). Because mortgagor is defined by s.205(1)(xvi) of the Act to include people deriving title under the original mortgagor, to comply with the first condition set out in the section, the mortgagee would have to serve notice on subsequent mortgagees. For this reason, this condition is frequently omitted in practice, which has the unfortunate effect that notice need not be served on the actual mortgagor (see (1986) Law Com. W.P. No. 99, para. 3.60).

In general terms the purchaser is not concerned to see that the power of sale has become exercisable (see LPA 1925, s.104(2)). The section further provides that any person damnified by an improper exercise of the power of sale shall have a remedy in damages against the person exercising the power of sale. The protection afforded by the statute is not, however, all embracing and there remains a role for general equitable principles to play in providing some protection for the mortgagor when an unauthorised sale of the mortgaged property occurs.

In *Jenkins* v *Jones* (1860) a mortgagee put the mortgaged property up for auction despite the mortgagor's having tendered the redemption money. This tender was repeated at the actual auction of the property but the purchaser nevertheless bid for it and the property was knocked down to him. It was held, in setting aside the sale, that the power of sale, as framed, relieved the purchaser from the need to make enquiries as to whether the sale was authorised. Where, however, as in this case, the purchaser was actually aware of circumstances which put the propriety of the sale into question and, despite that, proceeded with the purchase, then the transaction is liable to be set aside.

This decision did not involve statutory provisions regulating the exercise of the power of sale. However, a similar approach was taken to the effect of s.104 of the Act, admittedly *obiter*, in *Lord Waring* v *London and Manchester Assurance Co Ltd* (1935), where it was said by Crossman J that, "if the purchaser becomes aware ... of any facts showing that the power of sale is not exercisable, or that there is some impropriety in the sale, then, in my judgment, he gets no good title on taking the conveyance" ([1935] Ch 310 at 318).

The position therefore seems to be that a purchaser must ensure that the power of sale has arisen but need not make any enquiries as to whether the power has become exercisable. If, however, he is aware of facts which show that the power has not become exercisable, then he will not acquire a good title. Such an occurrence is likely to be very rare.

3. Proposals for reform

The law as it presently stands encourages the use of artificiality in mortgage deeds. In particular, the need for the purchase money to have become due, in order for the power of sale to arise, leads to the inclusion of a term in the mortgage that the sum borrowed will be repaid within six months of the date of the mortgage; a term that neither party expects to be complied with, and which serves only to make mortgage deeds more difficult to understand than is necessary. In a laudable attempt to simplify the law, the Law Commission has recommended legislation to alter the regulation of the mortgagee's exercise of the power of sale (see (1991) Law Com. No. 201). The principal recommendation with regard to this matter is to make the existence of the power of sale dependent on default by the mortgagor and to introduce a set procedure to be followed by the mortgagee, when seeking to sell the property. Furthermore, in the case of protected mortgages (which are defined essentially as mortgages of dwelling-houses), it is recommended that a court order would need to be obtained before a sale could be effected.

B. The exercise of the power of sale

1. The effect of the contract

When the mortgagee proceeds to exercise his power of sale, this will affect the ability of the mortgagor to redeem the mortgage. Thus in *Lord Waring* v *London and Manchester Assurance Co Ltd* (1935), the argument that the mortgagor could obtain an injunction to restrain the mortgagee from completing a contract of sale by tendering the redemption money was regarded as essentially untenable (see also *Property and Bloodstock Ltd* v *Emerton* (1968)); the result of entry into the contract of sale effectively suspended the mortgagor's equity of redemption, it no longer being possible for the mortgagor to redeem the mortgage.

A rather more difficult issue that can arise is where the mortgagor has contracted to sell the property and the mortgagee then exercises his power of sale. This occurred in *Duke* v *Robson* (1973). The first defendant, having contracted to purchase the beneficial interest of the second defendant, contracted to sell the property to the plaintiff. The mortgagee, who was the third defendant, then took possession of the property and contracted to sell it to the fourth defendant. The plaintiff then registered his contract as a land charge and sought specific performance of his contract to purchase and an injunction to restrain the completion of the contract between the third and the fourth defendants. The action failed, the Court of Appeal holding that the mortgagee was entitled to exercise his power of sale despite the existence of the earlier contract of sale which was regarded as a contract to sell merely the equity of redemption.

At first sight, the decision seems harsh, in that, as between the mortgagor and the plaintiff, the contract would be construed as a contract to sell an unencumbered fee simple and his inability so to do would render him liable in damages; such damages now potentially being substantial, following the abolition of the rule in *Bain* v *Fothergill* (1874) by s.3 of the Law of Property (Miscellaneous Provisions) Act 1989. On the other hand, it might be argued, if the mortgage was to be redeemed by the sale, the mortgagee's position would seem to be safeguarded and the action taken being calculated to do the maximum harm to the mortgagor.

On the facts of *Duke* v *Robson*, however, such criticism would be misplaced. Before the mortgagee exercised his power of sale, the mortgagor had not informed the mortgagee of the existence of the earlier contract of sale. Moreover, the mortgagor had neither given notice to redeem the mortgage nor had he purported to tender the redemption money. Had that been the case, then it would seem that the mortgagee would have been restrained from exercising his power of sale (see *Lord Waring* v *London and Manchester Assurance Co Ltd* (1935)). In cases where the mortgagor intends to sell the property and redeem the mortgage, he should, as a counsel of caution, first give the mortgagee notice of his intention to redeem (see also (1991) Law Com. No. 204, paras. 7.16-7.19).

2. Duties on sale

Next to consider are the duties that arise on the sale of mortgaged property. This is a complex matter involving a number of issues, such as the standard of care that must be exercised with regard to the purchase price that is obtained; the potential liability of agents involved in the sale and to whom any such liability might extend; the nature of the sale itself and the possible effect of exclusion clauses.

(a) Genuine sale
It has long been a recognised principle of equity that the mortgagee, in exercising his power of sale, cannot sell the property to himself.

This principle is applied also in cases of agency, it having been said in *Martinson* v *Clowes* that:

> "It is quite clear that a mortgagee exercising his power of sale cannot purchase the property on his own account, and I think it is clear also that the solicitor or agent of such mortgagee acting for him in the matter of sale cannot do so either." ((1882) 21 Ch D 857 at 860 *per* North J. See also *Downes* v *Grazebrook* (1817); *Whitcombe* v *Minchin* (1820)).

This principle will be applied in cases where a person purchases the property and then sells it on to the mortgagee, provided that this was a pre-planned transaction (see *Robertson* v *Norris* (1858)). Where the principle is applicable, the mortgagor, in seeking to set the transaction aside, need not show that it was fraudulent. Rather the rule is absolute:

> "A sale by a person to himself is no sale at all, and a power of sale does not authorise the donee of the power to take the property subject to it, even though such price be the full amount of the property." (*Farrar* v *Farrars Ltd* (1888) 40 Ch D 395 at 409 *per* Lindley LJ).

This principle was applied in *Williams* v *Wellingborough B.C.* (1975), where a local authority had sold a council house to the plaintiffs and had also granted them a mortgage. Subsequently, the authority purported to re-vest the property in itself, in consideration of the outstanding loan. The plaintiffs obtained an order that what had been done by the authority was void. This was because a mortgagee cannot sell the mortgaged property to itself.

The decision has since been reversed by legislation (Housing Act 1985, s.452 and Sched.17, replacing earlier legislation). This means that it is now possible for local authorities who have sold council houses to former tenants to buy the property back from them, if the purchasers later get into financial difficulties. A new tenancy can then be granted to them, thereby ensuring that the mortgagors do not become homeless. The general principle, however, that a mortgagee cannot sell the property to himself, remains intact (see, further, p. 75).

In the case of a sale to a related person or institution, the position is not as inflexible. If, for example, the mortgagee sells the property to a company with which he, or his family, is connected then that, of itself, is not sufficient to cause the sale to be set aside. The position is that the onus is on the mortgagee and the company to show that the sale was in good faith and that the mortgagee took reasonable precautions to obtain the best price reasonably obtainable at the time (see *Tse Kwok Lam* v *Wong Chit Sen* [1983] 1 WLR 1349 at 1355; *Farrar* v *Farrars Ltd* (1888)). If this onus can be discharged, the sale will be allowed to stand.

(b) Purchase price
In considering the duties of the mortgagee in respect of the purchase price obtained on the sale of the property, it is convenient to consider, first, the position of building societies, where this matter is regulated by statute, and then to consider the position as a matter of general law.

(i) Sales by building societies
The position of building societies, when exercising the power of sale, has been regulated by statute since 1939. The current position is governed by the Building Societies Act 1986 which imposes a duty, on selling the property, to take reasonable care that the price at which the land is sold is the best price that can reasonably be obtained. A further obligation imposed by the Act is, within 28 days of the sale, to send by recorded delivery to the mortgagor's last known address, a notice containing the prescribed details of the sale, together with a receipt. The information which must be given is as follows:
- the date of the mortgage deed under which the power of sale was exercised;
- the address or description of the property sold;
- the name and address of the vendor;
- the name and address of the purchaser and of any sub-purchaser, if this is known;
- the amount for which the property was sold;
- whether the sale was by private treaty or by public auction;
- the date of the completion of the sale.

(Building Societies (Supplementary Provisions as to

Mortgages) Rules 1986 (S.I. 1986 No. 2216)).

Any term in the agreement which seeks to contract out of these obligations is void (Building Societies Act 1986, s.13(7), Sched.4).

As will be seen, a similar duty has now been recognised to exist with regard to the purchase price in the case of sales by other mortgagees. The extent of the obligation placed on a building society may, however, be more onerous. In *Reliance Permanent Building Society* v *Harwood-Stamper* (1944) consideration was given to the predecessor of the current statutory provision. Vaisey J took the view that, subject to certain qualifications, the position of the building society should be equated with that of a trustee selling trust property ([1944] Ch 362 at 373). If this is the case then a building society would be under a duty to gazump, notwithstanding its own business ethics to the contrary, if a serious bid for the property, in excess of one already made, was received (see *Buttle* v *Saunders* (1950)). It is thought to be unlikely that other mortgagees would be regarded as being under such a duty and it is possible that, if the point arose, a building society may not be bound to accept the higher offer in these circumstances.

(ii) Sales by other mortgagees

The standard of care expected of mortgagees, who are not subject to any statutory obligation when exercising their power of sale, has been contentious for a considerable period. So, too, has the basis of that liability. The resolution of this latter issue, in particular, has had repercussions with regard to the question of who may sue in such cases and who may be sued.

It has long been established that a mortgagee is not a trustee of his power of sale and thus can exercise it having regard exclusively to his own interests. What for a long period was unclear was, in the exercise of the power, what duty was owed; the division of opinion being between those whose view was that the mortgagee need only act in good faith, and those who took the view that the mortgagee was under a duty to take reasonable care with regard to the purchase price.

Authority existed for both views. There were a number of cases where the judicial attitude to this question was that the mortgagee would not be liable provided that the power of sale was exercised in good faith (see, for example, *Kennedy* v *De Trafford* (1896); *Warner* v *Jacob* (1882); *Reliance Permanent Building Society* v *Harwood-Stamper* (1944)). Conversely, other decisions existed where the view had been expressed that the mortgagee was under a duty to exercise reasonable care to obtain the best price (see, for example, *McHugh* v *Union Bank of Canada* (1913); *National Bank of Australia* v *United Hand-in-Hand Band of Hope* (1879); *Farrar* v *Farrars Ltd* (1888); *Colson* v *Williams* (1889)). Against this background of conflicting authorities, the Court of Appeal had to decide *Cuckmere Brick Co* v *Mutual Finance Ltd* (1971).

In this case, the issue was whether the mortgagee was liable to the mortgagor in that, when the property was sold, there was no reference to the fact that the land to be sold had the benefit of planning permission to build flats on it, as opposed to merely building houses and, in consequence, the proper price had not been obtained as a result of negligence. In assessing this claim, therefore, the court had first to consider the ambit of the mortgagee's obligation to the mortgagor.

In undertaking this task, all three members of the Court of Appeal considered the authorities to be in a conflicting and unsatisfactory state but concluded that the standard of care to be imposed upon the mortgagee was to take reasonable care to obtain the true market or proper price. This was explained in the following terms:

> "The proximity beween them could hardly be closer. Surely they are 'neighbours'. Given that the power of sale is for the benefit of the mortgagee and that he is entitled to choose the moment to sell that suits him, it would be strange indeed if he were under no legal obligation to take reasonable care to obtain what I call the true market value at the date of the sale."
> ([1971] Ch 949 at 966 *per* Salmon LJ).

The significance of this decision was thought to be twofold. First, and most importantly, it resolved the thorny issue of what standard of care is to be imposed upon a mortgagee when exercising his power of sale; it now being settled that the duty is to take reasonable care to obtain the proper market price. Secondly, the reasoning employed to achieve this result seemed to indicate that the principles

THE SALE OF MORTGAGED PROPERTY

that govern this area are derived from the tort of negligence – a potentially significant matter in determining the possible ambit of the mortgagee's liability. As will be seen, however, this latter point is controversial.

Timing of sale: The traditional view is that, provided that the power of sale has become exercisable, the mortgagee owes no duty to the mortgagor as to when the property is sold. He need not wait until market conditions have improved before putting the property on the market (see *Davey* v *Durant* (1857) 1 De G & J 535 at 537; *Warner* v *Jacob* (1882) 20 Ch D 220 at 224; *Bank of Cyprus (London) Ltd* v *Gill* (1980)). So well entrenched was this view that it was said that the mortgagee would not be liable even if he sold the property to spite the mortgagor (*Nash* v *Eads* (1880) 25 SJ 95; *Belton* v *Bass, Ratcliffe & Gretton (Ltd)* [1892] 2 Ch 449).

After the decision in *Cuckmere*, it was felt that this view may need qualification. If the conduct of the sale was now governed by the principles of tort, then not only would the mortgagee be potentially liable in respect of the conduct of the sale but would also attract liability with regard to the timing of the sale. Any such liability would, however, be qualified significantly by the unquestioned right of the mortgagee to put his own financial interest ahead of that of the mortgagor.

This view attracted support in *Standard Chartered Bank Ltd* v *Walker*, where it was doubted whether the mortgagee could sell at the worst possible time and it was considered to be arguable that, in choosing when to sell, the mortgagee must exercise a reasonable degree of care ([1982] 1 WLR 1410 at 1415). These dicta were not cited, however, in *China and South Sea Bank Ltd* v *Tan Soon Gin* (1989), where a different view was taken.

In this case, shares had been mortgaged to secure a large loan. In addition to the mortgage, the mortgagee entered into a separate contract with the defendant who agreed to act as surety for the loan. At the time when payment was due, the value of the shares was sufficient to repay the loan. Subsequently, however, the shares became worthless and so the mortgagee brought an action against the surety. His defence was that, because the mortgagee had been negligent in not exercising its power of sale, he should not be held liable on the surety contract.

On the facts, it would not have been easy to establish negligence on the part of the mortgagee, the collapse of share prices not being easy to predict. The Privy Council, however, rejected the premise on which the argument was based, that the mortgagee owed the surety a duty of care with regard to the timing of the sale. Instead, the traditional view was reasserted that the mortgagee owes no duty to the mortgagor, and so by necessary implication to anyone else, with regard to when the property is sold so that the defendant was held liable on the surety contract. Although this approach has been criticised (see *Emmet on Title* (19th ed) para. 25.043), it is consistent with a general trend to limit liability in tort in respect of economic loss. For this reason, it is thought to be more likely to be followed than the different view expressed in *Standard Chartered Bank Ltd* v *Walker*.

Although it now seems to be clear that a mortgagee will not incur liability towards the mortgagor with respect to the timing of the sale, this does not mean that the mortgagor cannot influence this matter. In particular, the mortgagor may wish the property to be sold at an earlier date than the mortgagee, and to this end may petition the court under s.91(2) of the Law of Property Act 1925. Under this provision, in any action, whether for foreclosure, or for redemption, or for sale, or for the raising and payment in any manner of mortgage money, the court is empowered, on the request of the mortgagee or of any person interested either in the mortgage money or in the right of redemption, to direct a sale of the mortgaged property, notwithstanding that any other person dissents or that the mortgagee or any person so interested does not appear in the action.

The scope of this provision was considered in the important case of *Palk* v *Mortgage Services Funding plc* (1992). In this case, a mortgage of £300,000 was granted. Shortly afterwards the mortgagors fell into arrears with the repayments. In consequence a sale of the property was negotiated at a price of £283,000, that figure reflecting the slump in the property market. Meanwhile the mortgagee had obtained an order for possession, that order being suspended pending the hearing of an application by the mortgagors that

THE SALE OF MORTGAGED PROPERTY

the property be sold.

That application was opposed by the mortgagee, whose intention was to let the property and delay its sale until the housing market revived, which they anticipated would happen sooner or later. The problem with this from the point of view of the mortgagors was that the income that would be generated from any tenancy would be considerably less than the amount by which their indebtedness would increase as a result of the interest payable on the loan. The result of delaying a sale, therefore, would be that the mortgagors would be left owing considerably more to the mortgagee than was currently the case. An action could then subsequently be pursued under the covenant to repay with respect to any shortfall between the purchase price ultimately obtained and the amount of the debt that remained outstanding. To avoid this, a sale was sought even though the available price would not be sufficient to pay off the whole debt.

The Court of Appeal upheld this argument and ordered a sale, despite the mortgagee's objection. It was held that the effect of s.91(2) was to give the court a wide discretion as to what order to make. In the circumstances, to delay a sale would have caused considerable hardship to the mortgagors. On the other hand, a principal motivation of the mortgagee in taking the line it had was its commercial judgment that house prices would recover and so cause the property, in the end, to be a good security. It was held that the mortgagee could back its business judgment by purchasing the property itself. This would not transgress the principle that a mortgagee cannot sell the mortgaged property to himself because, if this course was adopted, the sale would be one that had been directed by the court.

It should be appreciated that this important decision does not abrogate from the principle that the mortgagee can sell the property at any time it chooses, subject, of course, to the power of sale having arisen and become exercisable. If, in this case, the matter had not been litigated, and the mortgagee had simply pursued its policy, then there would not have been liability to the mortgagor in respect of not exercising the power of sale. Neither does the decision mean that a mortgagee cannot, in general terms, obtain possession of the mortgaged property and create tenancies as a means of generating income from the property pending an eventual sale. Where such a course of action is proposed, however, and it would cause potential hardship to the mortgagor, then an application can be made by the mortgagor for the property to be sold.

Liability towards sureties: A person who acts as surety for the mortgagor has an obvious interest in the mortgagee exercising reasonable care in the exercise of the power of sale; in the event of the purchase price not realising the amount of the loan, he will be liable to make good the shortfall. At first, there was a judicial reluctance to hold that there was any duty of care between the mortgagee and a surety, the concern being that to recognise such liability would lead to a similar duty being owed to other creditors of the mortgagor (see *Barclays Bank Ltd* v *Thienel* (1978); *Latchford* v *Beirne* (1981)). These cases have since been disapproved in *Standard Chartered Bank Ltd* v *Walker* (1982) and *American Express International Banking Corp* v *Hurley* (1985) and it is now clear that such liability exists, a matter of some significance to insurance companies who may have provided cover extending to the payment of mortgages.

Liability to other parties: It was again thought that the duty owed to the surety stemmed from the close proximity between the parties and was thus a result of the application of tortious principles (see *Standard Chartered Bank Ltd* v *Walker* [1982] 1 WLR 1410 at 1415 *per* Lord Denning MR). It has now been held, however, that this is not the case and that the liability of the mortgagee will not be extended beyond the mortgagor and the surety.

In *Parker-Tweedale* v *Dunbar Bank plc* (1990) a wife was the mortgagor and her husband was a beneficial co-owner of the mortgaged property. After the mortgagee had exercised its power of sale, he sought to argue that it was liable to him, as a co-owner, for having sold the property at an undervalue, the basis of that liability being in tort. This was rejected. Nourse LJ said:

> "In my respectful opinion it is both unnecessary and confusing for the duties owed by a mortgagee to the mortgagor and the surety, if any, to be expressed in terms of the law of negligence" ([1991] Ch 12 at 18).

On this basis, it is now clear that the courts are not prepared to countenance the extension of the mortgagee's liability beyond the mortgagor and any surety. It will be noticed that in Nourse LJ's dictum some diffidence was apparent in whether any duty was, in fact, owed to a surety. It is thought, however, that in the light of the clear decisions accepting the existence of such a duty that this can now be regarded as settled. This duty arises, however, from equity: "Equity intervenes to protect a surety" (*China and South Sea Bank Ltd* v *Tan Soon Gin* [1990] 1 AC 536 at 544 *per* Lord Templeman, cited at [1991] Ch 12 at 19). It seems clear that this is the limit of the mortgagee's potential liability.

3. Extent of the duty

Having established the ambit of the mortgagee's duty when exercising his power of sale, it is now necessary to consider the situations when he may be held to be in breach of that duty, looking first at situations when the conduct of the sale is controlled by the mortgagee, and then considering the potential liability of the mortgagee for the conduct of agents employed by him. Finally attention will be turned to the question of whether there may exist liability directly between the mortgagee's agent and the mortgagor.

(a) Mortgagee's duty
The task of determining whether the mortgagee has fallen below the standard of care imposed upon him when exercising his power of sale is essentially one of fact. Despite that, certain illustrations may usefully be given of how liability may arise. An obvious source of liability is when the attributes of the property are not sufficiently indicated to potential purchasers, for example if the existence of planning permission is not properly indicated in situations where this would materially affect the purchase price (cf *Cuckmere Brick Co Ltd* v *Mutual Finance Co Ltd*. See also *American Express International Banking Corp* v *Hurley* (1985)).

Liability may also ensue as a result of the method of sale adopted. It may be thought that, if the sale is effected at a public auction, then the mortgagee would be safe from any subsequent action. This is not so. An auction may not be the most appropriate way of selling that particular type of property, so that a sale by this method may not secure the best market price (cf *Tse Kwok Lam* v *Wong Chit Sen* [1983] 1 WLR 1349 at 1356-1357 *per* Lord Templeman). The auction must also have been given adequate publicity and be conducted in proper conditions (see, for example, *Standard Chartered Bank Ltd* v *Walker* (1982); auction held in a cold and noisy room).

The essence of the mortgagee's responsibility is to ensure that the property is properly exposed to the market. An instructive decision is *Predeth* v *Castle Phillips Finance Co Ltd* ((1986), noted by MP Thompson [1986] Conv 442). The mortgagee, intending to exercise its power of sale, inspected the property and was shocked by its run-down condition. In consequence of what had been seen, the plan to put it into the hands of three estate agents was abandoned and agents were instructed to value the property on the basis of a "crash sale". Very shortly afterwards, the agents were contacted for a figure, in order that a sale could be concluded with a purchaser, with whom an agreement for sale had been reached, subject to contract. This transaction was subsequently completed at a slightly higher price than the valuation actually made, this being because another potential purchaser was showing interest in the property, and the property was resold shortly afterwards for a profit.

On these facts it was accepted that the mortgagee was liable to the mortgagor for the shortfall between the price actually obtained and that which should have been obtained. While it was not accepted that the fact that the property was subsequently resold at a profit would, of itself, indicate a failure to obtain the true market price, the instructions given to the agent indicated a desire to sell the property as soon as possible and, to accede to that instruction, the valuation given was lower than would have been the case if the sale had been conducted at a normal pace. Because it was accepted that the mortgagee was under a duty to expose the property fairly and properly to the market, the valuation on a "crash sale" basis amounted to a breach of that duty.

A matter which may come to be decided is whether a mortgagee may be in breach of his duty if he advertises the fact that the proper-

THE SALE OF MORTGAGED PROPERTY

ty to be sold is a repossessed property. The basis of this is that there is a common perception that such properties can be purchased for a reduced price and are seen as an opportunity to acquire a bargain. To avoid this potential problem, there is evidence that leading lending institutions take care to avoid publicising the fact that the property to be sold has been repossessed (see [1992] The Times 26 August). Much may depend on the facts of each case, but it is thought to be at least arguable that expressly advertising the property for sale as a repossessed property may amount to a breach of the mortgagee's duty to use reasonable care to obtain the best price for the property.

(b) Liability for agents

A normal practice for a mortgagee, when selling the mortgaged property, is to place the conduct of the sale in the hands of a reputable agent. The question that then arises is whether the mortgagee is liable for the default of the agent. It has long been settled that he is. In *Tomlin* v *Luce*, Collins LJ said:

> "The defence seems really to have been very much, if not entirely, directed to this, that the the first mortgagees selling under their power employed a competent auctioneer, and were not answerable for any blunder which the auctioneer committed. There they were wrong .... What we think is this, that the first mortgagees were answerable for any loss which was occasioned by the blunder made by their auctioneer at the sale." ((1889) 43 Ch D 191 at 194).

This proposition was also accepted in *Cuckmere Brick Co Ltd* v *Mutual Finance Ltd* and can now be taken as settled. In cases where the mortgagee is liable to the mortgagor because of the default of the agent, then he will normally be entitled to be indemnified by the agent. This is subject, first, to the terms of the contract between the mortgagee and the agent and, second, to the instructions that were given to the agent. Thus in *Predeth* v *Castle Phillips Finance Co Ltd*, the mortgagee failed in an action against the agent because the cause of the undervaluation of the property was its own instruction to value the property on a "crash sale" basis.

If the agent employed is an estate agent, or some such person, no problem arises in holding the mortgagee liable for any default by him. The position is a little more difficult where the sale is conducted by a receiver. Under s.109(2) of the Law of Property Act 1925, a receiver appointed under the Act is deemed to be the agent of the mortgagor and not the mortgagee. If the sale is conducted by him, and is at an undervalue, it might therefore be thought that the mortgagee will not be liable. If the sale is conducted by the receiver at the instigation of the mortgagee, however, then it was held in *American Express International Banking Corp* v *Hurley* (1985) that the receiver then becomes the mortgagee's agent and so he will then be liable.

(c) Liability of agents
A question that can arise is whether the agent who actually effects the sale can himself be directly liable to the mortgagor. In *Garland* v *Ralph Pay & Ransom* (1984), it was conceded that there could be such liability. Since that case was decided, however, there has been a marked reluctance, culminating in the leading case of *Murphy* v *Brentwood D.C.* (1990), to allow claims in negligence in respect of pure economic loss. A main concern, however, in limiting liability for pure economic loss is to prevent the spread of potentially wide-ranging liability. Such a consideration would not apply in the present context, and it is thought, given the very close proximity between the agent and the mortgagor, that an agent would still be regarded as potentially liable to the mortgagor.

If this proposition is correct, the existence of liability may well be affected by the instructions given to the agent by the mortgagee. In *Junior Books Ltd* v *Veitchi Co Ltd*, it was accepted that if A and B contract and B employs a sub-contractor C, then C will owe a duty of care to A. The scope of that duty is limited, however, by the terms of the contract between B and C (see [1983] 1 AC 520 at 546). Similarly, in the present context, if the agent implements the instructions of the mortgagee, and this causes loss to the mortgagor, the agent should not be liable. Where this is not the case, however, there seems to be no reason, in principle, why the agent should not be liable. Ordinarily, however, one would expect the mortgagor to bring his action against the mortgagee directly.

(d) Exclusion of liability

If the sale is by a building society, then – as has been seen – the society is precluded from excluding its statutory obligation (see p. 71). In the case of sales by other mortgagees, however, there is no such restriction on the ability to exclude or limit liability. Any clauses that seek to do this will, however, be construed strictly.

In *Bishop v Bonham* (1988) the mortgaged property consisted of shares. Clause three of the agreement provided that, on default in payment by the defendant, the plaintiff could sell the shares in any way he saw fit and that he would not be liable for any loss, howsoever caused. Clause eleven provided that the defendant would be bound to execute a transfer of the shares upon a sale by the plaintiff. A contract of sale was entered into but the defendant refused to execute a transfer, on the basis that he considered the sale price to be an undervalue. The plaintiff sought a summary order for specific performance but this was refused by the Court of Appeal, who gave the defendant leave to defend.

In reaching this conclusion, the court took the view that the relevant clauses were not drafted in such a way as to exclude all liability. The reference to a sale in any way the mortgagee saw fit was construed to mean in any way that complied with the general duty that the law imposes upon the mortgagee in exercising the power of sale, and the reference to loss, howsoever caused, was construed in the same way. Should a mortgagee seek to exonerate himself from the obligation to take reasonable care to obtain the proper market price, it is evident that a very clearly drafted clause will be necessary.

C. Effect of a sale

1. Position of purchaser

When the sale is effected under the mortgagee's statutory power, the position of the purchaser is itself governed by statute. Assuming that the power of sale has arisen, then the effect of a conveyance by the mortgagee is to vest in the purchaser the whole estate of the mortgagor, whether that estate is a fee simple or a term of years (Law of Property Act 1925, ss.98 and 99). The purchaser takes the property free from the mortgagor's equity of redemption and other subsequent mortgages, which are overreached, but subject to prior mortgages.

There is some doubt as to the position if the sale is by an equitable mortgagee. Again assuming that a deed has been employed to create the mortgage, so that the power of sale has arisen, the difficulty is that under the terms of the statutory provisions the mortgagee is empowered to sell "the mortgaged property", and in the case of an equitable mortgage this has been held to mean, in effect, the equity of redemption (see *Re Hodson and Howes Contract* (1887), but contrast *Re White Rose Cottage* (1965). See the discussion of this point in Megarry and Wade, *The Law of Real Property* (5th ed.) pp. 950-951). To circumvent this supposed problem, the methods used are either to employ a power of attorney, or to utilise a declaration of trust.

2. Proceeds of sale

It is clear that the mortgagee is not a trustee of the power of sale but, by virtue of s.105 of the Law of Property Act 1925, he is a trustee of the proceeds of sale. This section lays down how the proceeds are to be dealt with and in what order. The money must be applied as follows:
(a) in discharge of any prior incumbrance;
(b) in discharge of all costs, charges, and expenses properly incurred by him as incident to the sale or attempted sale;
(c) in discharge of the mortgage money, interest, and other money, if any, due under the mortgage; and
(d) the residue to the person entitled to the mortgaged property, or authorised to give receipts for the proceeds of sale thereof.

These provisions will be considered in turn.

THE SALE OF MORTGAGED PROPERTY

(a) Prior incumbrances
The requirement to discharge any prior incumbrances follows from the fact that the mortgagee cannot convey the property free from any mortgage having priority to his. This obligation will only arise, however, if the property was being sold free from such incumbrances.

(b) Expenses of the sale
The costs which are incidental to the sale obviously include such items as agent's fees and legal expenses. The expenses that can be recovered from the proceeds of sale extend more widely than that, and were recently reviewed in *Parker-Tweedale* v *Dunbar Bank (No. 2)* (1990).

In this case, the mortgagee sought to deduct the costs of the first action from the proceeds of sale realised by the sale of the mortgaged property. The first action had involved a claim by a beneficial owner that the mortgagee was liable to him for selling the property at an undervalue and had been dismissed with costs (see above). In refusing the application by the mortgagee, the Court of Appeal confirmed the existence of a general rule and an exception to it (see *Parker* v *Watkins* (1859)). The position was held to be that the mortgagee could obtain costs incurred in proceedings between him and a third party where what is impugned is the title to the estate itself, but cannot do so where the action relates either to the title of the mortgagee or to the exercise of its powers. Although recognising the position as illogical (see [1991] Ch 26 at 38 *per* Nourse LJ), it was nevertheless regarded as being well established with the result that, as the first action fell within the latter category, the attempt to add the costs of it to the security failed.

(c) Discharge of mortgage money
The mortgagee is entitled to retain from the proceeds of sale the money due. This includes arrears of interest, even if those arrears are statute-barred under the Limitation Act 1980 (*Re Lloyd* (1903)). The mortgagor is not allowed to claim any of the proceeds to satisfy any counterclaim he has against the mortgagee (*Samuel Keller (Holdings) Ltd* v *Martins Bank Ltd* (1970); *Mobil Oil Co Ltd* v *Rawlinson* (1982)).

REPOSSESSION OF PROPERTY ON MORTGAGE DEFAULT

(d) Residue

The Act provides that the residue is to be paid to the person entitled to the mortgaged property. Construed literally, this is the purchaser. To avoid this nonsensical result the Act is taken to refer to the person entitled to the mortgaged property before the sale. If there was only one mortgage over the property then the residue is paid to the mortgagor as representing his equity of redemption. Where this is not the case, then the mortgagee must pass the residue to the next subsequent mortgagee. On selling the property, therefore, the mortgagee should search either in the Land Charges Registry, if title is unregistered, or in the Land Registry, if title is registered, to discover if subsequent mortgages have been created. The mortgagee's duty is satisfied when he pays the money to the next mortgagee, who then himself holds the proceeds of sale on trust.

Chapter 4

Priorities of mortgages

When the mortgaged property has been sold, the question will arise as to who is entitled to the proceeds of sale. Where there has been only one mortgage of the property the solution is simple. After the mortgagee has taken what is owed to him, the balance of the purchase money should be paid to the mortgagor, this sum representing his equity of redemption. Where the property has been mortgaged more than once, however, the question of priorities as between the mortgagees will need to be addressed – a subject that is increasingly important in the light of the recent slump in the property market and the increasing incidence of situations where the level of mortgage debt on a property exceeds the value of the property itself (see Dorling, Gentle and Cornford, *Housing Crisis: Disaster or Opportunity,* University of Newcastle upon Tyne, Centre for Regional Development Studies, Discussion Paper No. 96, 1992). Further, there is the problem of establishing priorities in cases of mortgage fraud, where the same property has been mortgaged successively. This chapter considers the problems involved in determining the questions of priorities which can arise, in the context of both registered and unregistered land, including the position of both legal and equitable mortgages of the legal estate, and also including the subject of tacking.

Unfortunately, despite the major changes effected by the 1925 legislation, the law relating to this matter before that date can still be relevant and must be considered. Before considering these rules, it should also be pointed out that the mortgagees may, should they so wish, regulate the priorities, by agreement between themselves, regardless of whether the mortgagor consents (*Cheah Theam Swee* v *Equiticorp Finance Group Ltd* (1991)).

A. The law before 1925

The general law governing the issue of priorities of mortgages was encapsulated in two principles. These were that he that was first in time had the stronger case in law. Thus the general rule was that the mortgages ranked in order of their creation. Second, the principle was that where the equities were equal, the law prevailed. The application of these principles can best be seen by considering the various permutations that could arise and then considering the effect that the 1925 legislation has had upon the application of these principles.

1. Both mortgages legal

This position was unlikely to occur before 1925 because the method of mortgaging property before 1925 was to convey the fee simple to the mortgagee in return for the loan and have the property reconveyed upon redemption of the loan. Obviously, therefore, if this method of mortgage was employed, there could only be one legal mortgage of the property and this aspect of the priority problem could not arise. If, however, the mortgage was created by a long lease of the property, then a subsequent legal mortgage could be created by the grant of a second lease. The normal order of priority would then depend upon the order of the creation of the mortgages but, in principle, this would depend also upon the conduct of the first mortgagee with regard to the title deeds. This latter point may have continuing relevance to mortgages created after 1925, and normally was considered in situations which did not concern two legal mortgages. This issue can now be considered.

2. First mortgage legal; second mortgage equitable

The normal rule here was that the first mortgagee would have priority, the reasons being, first, that the mortgage was first in time and, second, that a legal mortgage is normally regarded as superior to an equitable mortgage. This priority could, however, be displaced in various situations.

(a) Fraud
It has long been accepted that if the first mortgagee is privy to any fraud by the mortgagor in creating subsequent mortgages, then priority will be lost. This was laid down in *Peter* v *Russell* (1716) (the *Thatched Cottage case*). In this case, the mortgagor of a lease borrowed the lease from the mortgagee, with whom it had been deposited, on the pretext that he needed it to enable him to sublet part of the land with a view to making improvements. In fact, he created a subsequent mortgage by depositing the lease with a second, innocent, mortgagee. It was held that the first mortgagee had not lost priority, because he was not a party to the fraud. Had he been, his mortgage would have been relegated to a position behind the subsequent equitable mortgagee. (See also *Evans* v *Bicknell* (1801) 6 Ves Jun 174 at 190 *per* Lord Eldon LC).

(b) Estoppel
As a matter of general principle, if the mortgagee permits the mortgagor to represent himself as the unencumbered owner of the property, with the result that a subsequent mortgagee is induced into lending on the security of the property, then the first mortgagee will be estopped from asserting priority (*Dixon* v *Muckleston* (1872) LR 8 Ch App 155 at 160 *per* Lord Selborne LC). Thus, for example, if a mortgagee indorses a receipt upon the mortgage, he will be estopped from denying that a subsequent equitable mortgagee, who has relied upon the receipt clause, has priority over the legal mortgage (*Rimmer* v *Webster* [1902] 2 Ch 163).

A good example of the operation of estoppel, in this context, is provided by *Perry-Herrick* v *Attwood* (1857). A voluntarily executed a mortgage in favour of his sisters to secure an antecedent debt.

They allowed him to retain the title deeds, so as to enable him to grant a security over the property to B. A deposited the deeds with B and then, without B's consent, obtained the deeds and created a further mortgage in favour of P. It was held that P's mortgage had priority over the legal mortgage held by the sisters. It was explained by Lord Cranworth LC, that "It is not a case in which there is any negligence. It is not a case, as I am willing to believe, in which there was any fraud, but it is a case in which the mortgagees did deliberately and intentionally leave the deeds in the hands of the mortgagor, in order that he might raise money" (1857) 2 De G & J 21 at 39).

Similarly, in *Briggs* v *Jones* (1870), B, a mortgagee of leasehold property, lent the lease to the mortgagor, in order that he could borrow further money by way of mortgage. Despite the mortgagor having been told by B that he should inform the new mortgagee of the existence of the prior mortgage, he did not do so. It was held that B had lost his priority.

It follows, therefore, that if the mortgagee allows the mortgagor to present himself as the unencumbered owner in order to raise further loans by mortgage, and the mortgagor does not inform the new mortgagee of the existence of the prior mortgage, then not only will mortgages that were envisaged by the first mortgagee have priority, but so will any other mortgages created by the mortgagor despite the ignorance of the first mortgagee. (For a dubious application of this principle, in a related context, see *Abbey National Building Society* v *Cann* [1991] AC 56 at 96 *per* Lord Oliver, criticised at [1992] Conv 206 at 210 (MP Thompson); and see above, pp. 54, 55).

(c) Gross negligence with regard to the deeds
A concept which, in the present context, is related to the role of estoppel, is the effect of gross negligence on the part of the mortgagee with regard to the title deeds. The similarity with the principle of estoppel is that the mortgagee enables the mortgagor to present himself as the unencumbered owner of the property; the difference is that this is not a deliberate act by the mortgagee: rather the issue relates to his culpability in not ensuring safe custody of the deeds. In considering this matter, there is some authority for the view that a different attitude is taken to the situation where the mortgagee fails

to obtain the deeds in the first place as opposed to the situation where he fails to retain them. Accordingly, these two situations will be considered separately.

(i) Failure to obtain the deeds

It has long been accepted that a legal mortgagee who fails to obtain the title deeds upon the creation of the mortgage runs the risk of losing priority to a subsequent equitable mortgagee. It is not, however, sufficient for the subsequent mortgagee to show that the prior legal mortgagee had not taken possession of the deeds; rather, "it must be shown that he left them in the hands of the mortgagor, either fraudulently, or what is called for want of a better expression, with gross negligence." (*Colyer* v *Finch* (1856) 5 HL Cas 905 at 924 *per* Lord Cranworth LC).

In cases where the mortgagee does not ask for the production of the deeds at all, then it is almost certain that priority will be lost to a subsequent mortgagee. In *Clarke* v *Palmer* (1882), P mortgaged various estates to M, but was allowed to retain the deeds. He then mortgaged one of the estates to AB, who obtained possession of the deeds relating to that estate. He then subsequently mortgaged all the estates to C. C advanced the money only after ascertaining the whereabouts of the deeds and satisfying himself, erroneously as it transpired, that AB was the only prior mortgagee. It was held that the order of priority was AB, C, and then M. The negligent failure of M to ask for the title deeds resulted in his loss of priority to the later mortgagees.

In *Clarke* v *Palmer*, the mortgagee lost priority because he had failed to ask for the deeds at all. It does not follow from this, however, that every failure to obtain the deeds will have this consequence. In *Grierson* v *National Provincial Bank of England Ltd* (1913), a mortgagor created an equitable mortgage of a lease, in favour of a bank, by deposit of title deeds. The mortgagor then created a legal mortgage, which was made expressly subject to the prior equitable mortgage in favour of the bank. The legal mortgagee did not, however, inform the bank of the existence of this mortgage. The mortgagor then redeemed the first equitable mortgage and so recovered the deeds. He then created another mortgage in favour of a second bank and the issue was whether the legal mortgagee, who never had had possession of the deeds, had lost priority to the bank. It was held that he had not, his failure to acquire the deeds not being regarded as sufficiently negligent to lose the *prima facie* priority of the legal estate.

The same principle applies to a failure to obtain all the deeds. In *Cottey* v *National Provincial Bank of England Ltd* (1904), the mortgagee's solicitor deceived the mortgagee into thinking that possession of the mortgage deed itself was sufficient, whereas the remaining deeds were then used by the mortgagor to create a second, equitable mortgage of the property. It was held that the mortgagee had not been guilty of gross negligence in relying upon his solicitor's advice and did not lose priority. Conversely, in *Walker* v *Linom* (1907), all the deeds to the property were taken, with the exception of the conveyance to the settlor. This was regarded as honest, but negligent, and the failure to acquire this deed led to the loss of priority. Much, therefore, will depend upon the facts of each case.

(ii) Failure to retain the deeds

The approach taken by the courts to the question of priorities, when the deeds have been obtained by the mortgagee who then subsequently loses possession of them, has been quite inconsistent. This is unfortunate in that, as will be seen, this question retains contemporary significance.

In *Northern Counties of England Fire Insurance Co* v *Whipp* (1884), C, the manager of a company, executed a mortgage of his own property to the company and deposited the deeds with them. The deeds were put into the company safe to which C, as manager, had a duplicate set of keys. Sometime later, C removed the deeds from the safe and deposited them by way of mortgage with W, who had no notice of the prior mortgage. It was held that the company had priority.

In reaching this conclusion, Fry LJ, who gave the judgment of the court, considered that there were two types of case that arose with regard to possession of the title deeds: cases where the mortgagee had not obtained the deeds in the first place and cases where he had done so, but subsequently had allowed them out of his possession. He took the view that, in determining whether priority had been lost by the prior legal mortgagee, the "two classes of cases will not be found to differ in the principles by which they are allowed to be governed, but they do differ much in the kind of fraud that is naturally looked for" ((1884) 26 Ch D 482 at 487). He then went on to say that "the Court will not postpone the prior legal estate to the subsequent equitable estate on the ground of any mere carelessness or want of prudence on the part of the legal owner" (*ibid.* at p. 494).

While it is true to say that the legal mortgagee has not been postponed to a subsequent equitable incumbrancer on the ground of mere carelessness with regard to possession of the deeds, the supposed distinction between a failure to obtain the deeds and a failure to retain them seems unfortunate and difficult to justify. The true principle would seem to be that stated by Lindley LJ, admittedly in the context of a dispute between an equitable mortgagee and a subsequent purchaser of a legal estate, that:

"to deprive a man of the protection of the legal estate he must have been guilty of either fraud or gross negligence. To deprive a purchaser for value without notice of the protection of the legal estate it is not, in my opinion, essential that he should have been guilty of fraud; it is sufficient that he has been guilty of such gross negligence as would render it unjust to deprive the prior incumbrancer of his priority" (*Oliver* v *Hinton* ([1899] 2 Ch 264 at 274).

By analogy, it is submitted that the test to be applied in determining whether a prior legal incumbrancer should lose his priority is the same: has he behaved with a sufficient degree of negligence so as to render it unjust for him to rely upon the protection of the prior legal estate – and that this test is equally applicable if the culpability of the mortgagee relates to a failure to obtain the deeds or to a failure to retain them. Indeed, from the perspective of the subsequent mortgagee, it is difficult to see that the distinction has any validity. It may also be the case that the supposed distinction is based upon situations where the deeds were deposited with a person standing in a fiduciary position to the mortgagee, so that the failure to retain the deeds is far less culpable than a failure to acquire them in the first place (see *Walker* v *Linom* [1907] 2 Ch 104 at 118 *per* Parker J). It is submitted, therefore, that a mortgagee who releases the deeds for an inadequate reason, or who fails to exercise a proper degree of care to ensure their safekeeping, is at risk of his mortgage being postponed to a subsequent mortgagee.

3. First mortgage equitable; second mortgage legal

In a contest between a prior equitable mortgage and a subsequent legal mortgage, one would anticipate that the position would be straightforward: the question of priority would be determined by considering, simply, whether the legal mortgagee had notice of the prior equitable mortgage. If he did, the equitable mortgagee would have priority; if he did not, then as a bona fide purchaser of the legal estate without notice, he would take free of the equitable interest and, therefore, have priority over it (see *Pilcher* v *Rawlins* (1872)). Matters are not, however, resolved on this basis.

For reasons that have never been clearly articulated, the courts have resolved this issue by considering whether the subsequent legal mortgagee has been grossly negligent in not obtaining the title deeds. The point about this is that the failure of the mortgagor to be able to produce the deeds should put the mortgagee on notice that they have been deposited elsewhere, for the purpose of securing a loan.

The approach taken, however, is to investigate the reason accepted by the legal mortgagee for the non-production of the deeds. This was explained, as follows, in *Hewitt* v *Loosemore* (1851):

"The law ... stands thus: That a legal mortgagee is not to be postponed to a prior equitable one upon the ground of his not having got in the title-deeds, unless there is fraud or gross and wilful negligence on his part. That the court will not impute fraud, or gross or wilful negligence to the mortgagee if he has bona fide inquired for the deeds, and a reasonable excuse has been given for the non-delivery of them; but that the court will impute fraud, or gross and wilful negligence to the mortgagee if he omits all inquiry as to the deeds." ((1851) 9 Hare 449 at 458 *per* Sir George Turner V-C. See also *Oliver* v *Hinton*

[1899] 2 Ch 264 at 274 *per* Lindley LJ).

Consistent with this approach, the courts will accord priority to the equitable mortgagee when the subsequent legal mortgagee has not enquired at all as to the whereabouts of the deeds. If he has made enquiries and accepted an explanation for their non-production, seemingly however feeble, such as that they were in Ireland (see *Agra Bank Ltd* v *Barry* (1874)), then the legal mortgagee will have priority. It is difficult to reconcile this rather relaxed approach to the protection of equitable interests with that which is generally adopted, but the principle is well established.

4. Equitable mortgage followed by another equitable mortgage

In determining the issue of priority between equitable mortgagees, "the question is whether one party has acted in such a way as to justify him in insisting on his equity as against the other" (*National Provincial Bank of England* v *Jackson* (1886) 33 Ch D 1 at 13 *per* Cotton LJ). The general rule is that the first in time will prevail. For this rule to be displaced, the first mortgagee must have been negligent with regard to the custody of the title deeds. It is probably the case that a lesser degree of negligence will suffice than that which is required for a prior legal mortgagee to lose his priority (*Taylor* v *Russell* [1892] AC 244 at 262 *per* Lord Macnaghten, doubting the opinion to the contrary of Kay J in the same case at first instance: [1891] 1 Ch 8 at 15).

B. The law after 1925

The rules regulating the priority of mortgages, as developed by the courts, have been modified substantially by the 1925 legislation (see, generally, RE Megarry (1940) 7 CLJ 243). These rules have not, however, been totally supplanted and, as will be seen, continue to have relevance to some situations that may arise. Consideration will first be given to unregistered land and then to the position when title has been registered.

1. Unregistered land

After 1925, a mortgage is no longer created by conveying the land to the mortgagee, with the land being re-conveyed upon the redemption of the mortgage. Consequently, it is now commonplace for more than one legal mortgage to be created of the same property. For this reason, certain legal mortgages, as well as equitable mortgages, were made registrable as a land charge. The main issues to consider are whether a particular mortgage is registrable and the operation of the registration provisions.

A distinction is made between a mortgage that is protected by deposit of title deeds and one that is not. In the case of the former category of mortgage, the mortgage is not registrable, whereas the latter type of mortgage is registrable as a land charge.

(a) Registrable mortgages
A mortgage which is protected by deposit of title deeds is excluded from any category of land charge (although see below). This is slightly unfortunate, in that, while it is acceptable that a mortgage which is protected in this manner should be sufficiently protected by that fact alone, there seems to be no good reason to preclude such a mortgagee from being able to register, should he so desire, out of an abundance of caution.

It is generally accepted that "protected by deposit of title deeds" means a mortgage that is originally protected by deposit of deeds, so that a mortgage that is originally protected does not become registrable if the mortgagee relinquishes the deeds. The opposite view would mean that such a mortgage would oscillate between being registrable and non-registrable, depending upon the current whereabouts of the deeds. It should therefore follow, as a matter of general principle, that, if the mortgagee negligently parts with the deeds, then priority may be lost to a subsequent mortgagee. The rules relating to the consequences of a failure to obtain the deeds at all are no longer applicable, because a mortgage which is not protected by deposit of title deeds is now registrable and the question of priority is now governed by the legislative provisions governing registration.

(b) Non-registrable mortgages
A mortgage which is not protected by deposit of title deeds is registrable as a land charge. In the case of a legal mortgage, such a mortgage, which is termed a puisne mortgage, is registrable as a class C(i) land charge (Land Charges Act 1972, s.2(4)(i)). The position of an equitable mortgage which is protected by a deposit of title deeds is, unfortunately, a little more complicated.

Prima facie, an equitable mortgage seems to come within the definition of a class C(iii) land charge, as defined by s.2(4)(iii) of the Land Charges Act 1972. This provides as follows:
A general equitable charge is any equitable charge which –
(a) is not protected by a deposit of title deeds relating to the legal estate affected; and
(b) does not arise or affect an interest arising under a trust for sale or a settlement; and
(c) is not a charge given by way of indemnity against rents equitably apportioned or charged exclusively on land in exoneration of other land and against breach or non-observance of covenants or other conditions; and
(d) is not included in any other class of land charge.
The difficulty lies in the final paragraph. Although it seems likely that any mortgage, be it legal or equitable, was intended to depend for its priority on the fact of the deposit of the deeds, in the case of an equitable mortgage this may not be the case. This is because an equitable mortgage created by a deposit of title deeds would seem to fall within the definition of an estate contract and so be registrable as a class C(iv) land charge, this class of land charge being defined to include a contract by an estate owner, or by any person entitled at the date of the contract to have a legal estate conveyed to him, to convey or create a legal estate (Land Charges Act 1972, s.2(4)(iv)).

The basis of an equitable mortgage created by a deposit of title deeds has traditionally been seen as an imperfect method of creating a legal mortgage. As such, it was treated in the same way as any other attempt to create a legal interest in land: as a contract to create the equivalent interest. Provided that the contract was specifically enforceable, equity would regard that which ought to be done as already having been done and view the transaction as an equitable mortgage (see *Russel* v *Russel* (1783)). On this basis, therefore, an equitable mortgage would seem to be registrable as an estate contract.

As against this view, it may be argued that an equitable mortgage should now be regarded as having a validity independent from its original theoretical basis. This argument may gain additional force when considering the question of formalities. Prior to the coming into force of s.2 of the Law of Property (Miscellaneous Provisions) Act 1989, a contract for the sale of land, or any interest in land, was enforceable provided that there was a sufficient note or memorandum of the contract or a sufficient act of part performance of it (Law of Property Act 1925, s.40(1) and (2)). In the case of an equitable mortgage by deposit of title deeds, the act of depositing the deeds was regarded as an act of part performance by both parties – an unusual finding in the law of part performance. Since the coming into force of the 1989 Act, which abolished the doctrine of part performance, such a justification is untenable. It may nevertheless be the case, however, that the courts will continue to recognise such a deposit as having created an equitable mortgage (see Megarry's *Manual of the Law of Real Property* (7th ed.) p. 446, although compare the rather cautious approach in *Emmet on Title* para. 25.116). If this view is correct, then an equitable mortgage could properly be regarded as being outside both the definition of a general equitable charge and an estate contract and, therefore, not registrable. Although such a conclusion seems preferable, the matter is not clear and, therefore, as a counsel of caution such a mortgage should be registered as an estate contract (see, further, Megarry and Wade, *The Law of Real Property* (5th ed.) pp. 998, 999, where the view is taken that such mortgages are not registrable – a view which seems preferable to the alternative).

An equitable mortgage which is not protected by a deposit of title deeds clearly falls within the definition of a general equitable charge and is therefore registrable as a class C(iii) land charge.

(c) Both mortgages protected
It is possible, but unlikely, that both mortgages will be protected by deposit of title deeds. This is possible if the first mortgagee mistak-

enly thinks that he has been given all the deeds and then the remaining deeds are deposited with the second mortgagee. In this situation, the priorities are governed by the pre-1925 rules and the first mortgagee will have priority, as first in time. If the first mortgagee originally has the title deeds, but then relinquishes them, then that mortgage will remain unregistrable. If a second mortgage is then created, the title deeds being deposited with the second mortgagee, then, as indicated above, the issue of priority will be determined by whether the first mortgagee was grossly negligent in his failure to retain them. The position, again, is governed by the pre-1925 rules.

(d) Both mortgages registrable
This situation will arise when neither mortgagee has possession of the title deeds. The resulting issue of priority will then be determined by the interrelation of two statutory provisions which, unfortunately, do not always complement each other. The relevant provisions are s.97 of the Law of Property Act 1925 and s.4(5) of the Land Charges Act 1972.

Section 97 provides that:
> Every mortgage affecting a legal estate in land made after the commencement of this Act, whether legal or equitable (not being a mortgage protected by the deposit of documents relating to the legal estate affected) shall rank according to its date of registration as a land charge pursuant to the Land Charges Act [1972].

Section 4(5) of the Land Charges Act 1972 provides that:
> A land charge of ... Class C (other than an estate contract) created or arising after 1st January 1926 shall be void as against a purchaser of the land charged with it, or of any such interest in such land, unless the land charge is registered in the appropriate register before the completion of the purchase.

The interrelation of the provisions can be seen by considering various possible situations.

(i) Registration of prior mortgage
The situation envisaged is where the first unprotected mortgage is registered and then the second mortgage is created, it being immate-

rial whether the second mortgage is or is not protected by deposit of title deeds. In every case, the first mortgagee will have priority, irrespective of whether either or both mortgages are legal or equitable. If neither mortgage is protected, the first mortgage will have priority both because it is the first to be registered and also because the second mortgagee is deemed to have notice of it because of its registration (Law of Property Act 1925, s.198). If the second mortgage is protected, then the first mortgage will still have priority as the second mortgagee will have taken the mortgage with notice of the prior mortgage.

(ii) Non-registration of prior mortgage
In this situation the first mortgage is unregistered and the second mortgage is either protected by deposit of title deeds or is unprotected but registered as a land charge. In both situations the second mortgagee has priority. In the case of the second mortgage being protected then, under s.4(5) of the Land Charges Act 1972, the first mortgage is void against him as a purchaser of any interest in the land without notice. It is, therefore, immaterial if the second mortgage is legal or equitable. If the second mortgage is registered before the first mortgage, then the second mortgagee has priority for two reasons: (i) under the Land Charges Act 1972, the first mortgage is void against the second mortgagee for non-registration, and (ii) under s.97 of the Law of Property Act 1925, the second mortgage has priority as the first to be registered.

(iii) Both mortgages registered
When both mortgages are registered as land charges, considerable difficulty can ensue. The following is a typical set of circumstances:

    January 1:   A grants a mortgage to X.
    January 5:   A grants a mortgage to Y.
    January 10:   Y registers.
    January 11:   X registers.

In this situation the two statutory provisions conflict to create an impasse. Under the Land Charges Act, the order of priority would be X then Y. This is because X's mortgage is void against Y for non-registration. Under the Law of Property Act, the order of priority is

Y then X, because under the terms of s.97, the mortgages rank in order of their registration.

Support exists for both solutions. In favour of the first is the argument that it is difficult to see how something that is void for non-registration can be resuscitated, as it were, by the expedient of subsequently registering it (cf *Kitney* v *MEPC Ltd* (1977). See, for example, Megarry and Wade *op cit* pp. 1000, 1001). As against this, there is the argument that s.97 does deal explicitly with the question of the priorities of mortgages and that, therefore, in the event of conflict between it and the more general ambit of the Land Charges Act, it should prevail. Indeed, it is otherwise difficult to see what function is performed by the section as other problems of priority can be resolved without resort to it (see *Emmet on Title* para. 25.103).

Despite the strength of this latter argument, it is suggested that the solution arrived at by the application of s.4(5) of the Land Charges Act 1925 is to be preferred and is the one most likely to be adopted. This is for the practical reason that the first mortgagee was in a position to protect his interest by registration, whereas the second mortgagee could not have discovered the existence of the first mortgage and, moreover, would have relied upon a clear certificate of search. It is, perhaps, not wholly unreasonable to equate the position of X, the first mortgagee, who has failed to register his mortgage, with that of a legal mortgagee who, before 1925, was guilty of gross negligence in not obtaining the title deeds, thereby enabling the mortgagor to present himself as owner of an unencumbered estate and, as a result, losing priority. The position is as yet judicially unresolved, as are the even more intractable problems that can be constructed where three mortgages are involved (see Megarry and Wade *op cit* pp. 1001, 1002, suggesting that the solution lies in subrogation).

(iv) Priority notices and searches

A mortgagee, who is contemplating lending money on the security of an unprotected mortgage, can obviate the problems discussed above by registering a priority notice. Under this procedure, the mortgagee should register a priority notice not less than fifteen working days before the creation of the mortgage. He must then apply for substantive registration of the charge not more than thirty days after the mortgage was created. This then has the effect that the date of the registration is deemed to be the date of the mortgage, thereby ensuring that there can be no prior registration (Land Charges Act 1972, s.11(1), (2) and (3)). The reason that the period of fifteen days is specified is that that is the period of priority given to the conclusiveness of an official certificate of search, so that any land charge registered against an estate owner, during that period of grace, is ineffective in so far as a person who has obtained a clear certificate of search against that estate owner and who completes within that period is concerned (Land Charges Act 1972, s.11(5)). Any person contemplating lending by way of mortgage should, of course, requisition an official search of the land charges register.

2. Registered land

In considering the issue of the priority of mortgages of registered land, three types of case must be considered. These are where there exist registered charges; where there are protected minor interests; and where there are unprotected minor interests. It should be noted that, under s.106(2) of the Land Registration Act 1925, the position is that unless and until a mortgage becomes a registered charge it takes effect only in equity.

(a) Registered charges

The issue of priority of registered charges is governed by s.29 of the Land Registration Act 1925, which provides that, subject to any entry to the contrary on the register, registered charges on the same land shall as between themselves rank according to the order in which they are entered on the register, and not according to the order in which they are created.

In situations where there may be more than one charge, the priority of a mortgagee can be protected by his obtaining an official search with priority under rule 6 of the Land Registration (Official Searches) Rules 1990 (S.I. 1990 No. 1361). Under rule 6, any entry that is made in the register during the priority period relating to that

search (a period of thirty working days) shall be postponed to a subsequent application to register the purchase, provided that the mortgagee's application to register the mortgage as a legal charge is:
  (a) deemed to have been delivered at the proper office within the priority period;
  (b) affects the same land or charge as the postponed entry; and
  (c) is in due course completed by registration.
Where two official searches are made with priority then, under rule 8, the priority between them is, unless the parties agree otherwise, in the order that the applications were made.

(b) Protected minor interests
As noted above, a mortgage, until registered as a legal charge, can only take effect as a minor interest. As such, it can be protected by either a caution or a notice (Land Registration Act 1925, s.106(2)). If so registered, it will have priority over any subsequent interest, be it a registered charge or an unregistered charge. If it is not registered, it will not be binding upon a subsequent registered chargee (Land Registration Act 1925, s.20).

(c) Unprotected minor interests
If neither mortgagee has registered the mortgage as a registered charge, then both mortgages take effect only in equity. As such, the contest is one for priority between two competing equitable interests and this conflict is resolved by the application of general equitable principles. It follows, therefore, that the normal rule is that the first in time should have priority. This rule is unaffected by registration. Thus, in *Barclays Bank Ltd* v *Taylor* (1974), it was held that an equitable mortgagee had priority over purchasers, who had yet to be registered as proprietors but had protected their contract by the registration of a caution, on the basis that the contest was between two equitable interests and the first in time prevailed, notwithstanding the registration of the latter interest.

It has subsequently been argued that this decision should be distinguished if the holder of the second equitable interest had been a mortgagee, rather than a purchaser, or if the method of protection had been by registration of a notice, rather than by registration of a caution (see also, on the latter point, Fairest, *Mortgages* (2nd ed.) pp. 150, 151). Happily, both these arguments were rejected in *Mortgage Corporation Ltd* v *Nationwide Credit Corporation Ltd* ([1992] The Times 27 July), and the general position that, as between two competing equitable interests, the first in time will prevail was reaffirmed.

This is not to say that registration may not be relevant in the resolution of these issues. A prior mortgagee who takes no steps to protect the mortgage may lose priority to a subsequent mortgagee on the basis of gross negligence – a failure to take any steps at all to protect the mortgage being likely to be regarded in this way. Thus in *Barclays Bank Ltd* v *Taylor*, the Court of Appeal declined to interfere with the normal rule regarding priority, because the bank, which was in possession of the land certificate, a fact noted on the register, had not conducted itself in a way that would justify postponement of its equity (see [1974] Ch 137 at 147 *per* Russell LJ. Similar observations were also made in *Mortgage Corporation Ltd* v *Nationwide Credit Corporation Ltd*, above). If the first mortgagee takes no steps to protect the mortgage, either by registration of a caution or a notice, or by possession of the land certificate, then priority may well be lost to a subsequent mortgage which is itself not registered as a legal charge.

C. Tacking

Tacking is the process whereby a mortgagee can obtain priority over other interests in the land, prior to his, by the process of tacking the mortgage to a pre-existing mortgage which has priority over those other interests, thereby altering the priorities which would otherwise exist. Put another way, the mortgagee can make further advances to the mortgagor on the basis of the original security, notwithstanding the existence of other mortgages created after the original mortgage.

Before 1926, there existed two forms of tacking. These were:
(i) the *tabula in naufragio* (the plank in the shipwreck); and
(ii) the tacking of further advances.

PRIORITIES OF MORTGAGES

The former doctrine was abolished, in so far as the priorities of mortgages is concerned, by s.94(3) of the Law of Property Act 1925. It may continue to be relevant in working out the priorities of other competing interests, such as an option to purchase (see, for example, *McCarthy & Stone Ltd* v *Julian S Hodge & Co Ltd* (1971)). Such issues are, however, beyond the scope of this book. (See Megarry and Wade *op cit* pp. 1006-1008).

1. Tacking of further advances

The situation when a mortgagee can tack a subsequent loan to a pre-existing mortgage is governed by s.94 of the Law of Property Act 1925. A mortgagee is now permitted to tack in three situations.

(a) Agreement of intervening mortgagee
Little need be said about this head. If A has mortgaged his property first to X and then to Y, and wishes to borrow more money against the security of the property, X may be willing and able to advance the money, whereas Y may not. In this case, provided, of course, that Y agrees, the further loan may be tacked to the first.

(b) No notice of intervening mortgages
Under s.94(1)(b) of the Law of Property Act 1925, any mortgagee can tack if he did not have notice of the existence of an intervening mortgage. If the property is mortgaged first to X and then to Y, and Y has possession of the title deeds, then X has notice of the intervening mortgage and may not tack any further advance to the first mortgage. Similarly, if Y does not have possession of the title deeds, but protects the mortgage by the registration of a land charge, again X has notice and therefore cannot tack.

If, however, the original mortgage in favour of X is made for securing a current account or for securing further advances, then the rules as to notice are modified. In this case, it is provided by s.94(2) of the Law of Property Act 1925 that a mortgagee shall not be deemed to have notice of the intervening mortgage merely by reason of its having been registered as a land charge, if it was not so registered when the original mortgage was created or when the last search by, or on behalf of, the mortgagee was made, whichever was the latest. The position with regard to deposit of title deeds is unaffected. A second mortgagee who does not have possession of the title deeds, should always, therefore, serve notice of the existence of his mortgage upon the first mortgagee to avoid tacking taking place under this head.

A further exception to the general rule that registration of a land charge constitutes actual notice is made, in the present context, with regard to a spouse's statutory right of occupation. Section 2(10) of the Matrimonial Homes Act 1983 similarly provides that where a mortgage is in existence before the registration of the statutory right of occupation, then – for the purposes of s.94 of the Law of Property Act 1925 – the statutory right is to be regarded as a subsequent mortgage. The effect of this is that the mortgagee may tack any further advance to the original loan.

Some caution is necessary, however. If the spouse or, indeed, other cohabitee is in occupation of the property as a beneficial co-owner, then the mortgagee will not be able to tack any further advance to the original loan. In such circumstances, the mortgagee may find that the full amount of the loans to the mortgagor is not secured, as against the co-owner, in that her interest may have priority over the security taken for the second advance (cf *Equity and Law Home Loans Ltd* v *Prestidge* (1991), and see Chapter 2). In this event, although the mortgagee will be able to sell the property, the co-owner will be entitled to have her beneficial share satisfied from the proceeds of sale before the mortgagee can recover the amount of the further advance.

(c) Obligation to make further advance
A mortgagee may tack a further advance to the original mortgage if it is a term of that mortgage that he must make further advances. In this event, it is immaterial if the mortgagee has notice of any intervening mortgages.

2. Registered land

Where title to the land is registered, the right to tack is governed by s.30 of the Land Registration Act 1925. Under this section, only a registered chargee has the right to tack. Where the proprietor of a charge is under an obligation, noted on the register, to make further advances, any further charge shall take effect subject to any further advance made pursuant to that obligation.

Where the proprietor of the charge is not obliged to make further advances, but it is made for securing further advances, then before making any entry on the register that would prejudicially affect the priority of any further advances that may be made, the registrar must give notice of it to the registered proprietor of the charge. The entry will not then affect the proprietor of the charge unless it was made after the notice should have been received in due course by post. If the proprietor of the charge suffers loss by reason of any failure of the registrar or the Post Office, he is entitled to an indemnity as if the mistake had been made by the registrar.

Index

Administration orders, effect of 5-9
Adoption by mortgagee of unauthorised tenancies 29, 34-35
Agents, conduct of sale by:
    liability in respect of...80
    liability of mortgagee for default of agents 79-80

Beneficial interest, acquisition of a 37-49
    constructive trust, under a 42-46
        agreement to share the beneficial ownership...................................44-46
        contribution to the acquisition of the property...................................43-44
    equitable estoppel, under the doctrine of 46-49
        satisfying the estoppel..48-49
    express trust, under an..37-38
    resulting trust, under a 38-42
        direct contributions 40-41
        indirect contributions 41-42

Co-owners, beneficial, effect of on mortgagee 36-61
    acquisition of a beneficial interest...37-49
        constructive trust, under a..42-46
        equitable estoppel, under the doctrine of..46-49
        express trust, under an 37-38
        resulting trust, under a 38-42
    priority of rights as against mortgagee...50-61
        Boland, limitations on..53-61
        registered land..50-52
        unregistered land 52
    See also *Co-owners, legal, effect of consent of*
Co-owners, legal, effect of consent of...55-61
    forgery of signature, effect of..56-57
    vitiating factors to consents...57-61
        agent of mortgagee, effect of finding of borrower as 57-58
        undue influence to procure signature, exercise of 58-61

REPOSSESSION OF PROPERTY ON MORTGAGE DEFAULT

Dwelling-houses, statutory restrictions on mortgagee's right to possession of – see *Restrictions on possession*

Extortionate credit bargains 20-22

Insolvent corporate mortgagors, enforcement of security against 5-9

Jurisdiction of county court 2

Leases – see *Tenancies, effect of on mortgagee*
Liabilities of mortgagee in possession 24-25
    rents and profits, in respect of 25-27
    repairs and improvements, in respect of 25
    See also *Receiver, appointment of*

Mortgage rescue schemes 24

Possession, mortgagee's right to 1-2
    liabilities of mortgagee in possession 24-25
        rents and profits, in respect of 25-27
        repairs and improvements, in respect of 25
    See also *Receiver, appointment of*
    restrictions on mortgagee's right 3-22
        attornment clauses 4-5
        dwelling-houses, statutory restrictions in respect of 9-22
        insolvent corporate mortgagors, statutory restrictions in respect of 5-9
        mortgage deed, qualifications in 3-4
    See also *Resisting possession proceedings*
Postponement of possession – see *Restrictions on possession; Resisting possession proceedings*
Price, mortgagee's duties in respect of obtaining best 70-81
    building societies, sales by 70-71
    liability of agents 80
    liability of mortgagee 77-79
        agents, for default of 79-80
        exclusion clauses 81
        sureties, towards 76-77
    other mortgagees, sales by 71-73
    timing of sale 73-76
Priorities of mortgages – the law after 1925 93-102
    registered land 100-102
        protected minor interests 101
        registered charges 100-101
        unprotected minor interests 101-102
    unregistered land 94-100
        both mortgages protected by deposit of title deeds 96-97

INDEX

both mortgages registrable 97-100
non-registrable mortgages 95-96
priority notices, registration of 99-100
registrable mortgages 94
Priorities of mortgages – the law before 1925 86-93
both mortgages legal 86
equitable mortgage followed by another equitable mortgage 93
first mortgage equitable; second mortgage legal 92-93
first mortgage legal; second mortgage equitable 87-92
deeds, loss of priority as a result of failure to obtain 89-90
deeds, loss of priority as a result of failure to retain 90-92
estoppel, loss of priority as a result of 87-88
fraud by mortgagor, loss of priority as a result of 87
Priority of rights as between beneficial co-owners and mortgagees 50-61
Boland, limitations on 53-61
first mortgages 53-55
legal co-ownership 55-61
registered land 50-52
unregistered land 52
See also *Co-owners, beneficial, effect of on mortgagee*
Proceeds of sale, application of 82-84
expenses incurred, discharge of 82, 83
mortgage money, discharge of 82, 83
prior incumbrances, discharge of 82, 83
residue 82, 84
See also *Priorities of mortgages*

Receiver, appointment of 27-29
advantages of 28-29, 35
Rents and profits, liabilities of mortgagee in possession in respect of 25-27
Repairs and improvements, liabilities of mortgagee in possession in
respect of 25
Rescheduling of mortgage repayments 22-23
Resisting possession proceedings 22-24
mortgage rescue schemes 24
rescheduling of mortgage repayments 22-23
social security payments to mortgagee 23-24
Restrictions on possession 3-22
attornment clauses 4-5
dwelling-houses, statutory restrictions in respect of 9-22
Administration of Justice Act 1970, s.36 10-12
Administration of Justice Act 1973, s.8 12-15
Consumer Credit Act 1974, postponement of possession under 19-22
factors influencing exercise of court's power to postpone 17-19
Matrimonial Homes Act 1983, protection of mortgagor's
spouse under 16-17

    Practice Direction 1991 15-16
    insolvent corporate mortgagors, statutory restrictions in respect of 5-9
    mortgage deed, qualifications in 3-4
    See also *Resisting possession proceedings*

Sale of mortgaged property by mortgagee 62-84
    duty of care in respect of the sale 77-81
        agents, liability of to mortgagor 80
        agents, mortgagee's liability for default of 79-80
        exclusion of liability 81
        mortgagee's liability 77-79
    effect of contract of sale 67-68
    genuine sale, mortgagee's duties in respect of 68-70
    power of sale arising 62-64
        deed, mortgage must have been made by 63
        due, purchase money must have become 63-64, 66
    power of sale becoming exercisable 65-66
    proceeds of sale 82-84
        expenses incurred, discharge of 82, 83
        mortgage money, discharge of 82, 83
        prior incumbrances, discharge of 82, 83
        residue 82, 84
    See also *Priorities of mortgages*
    purchase price, mortgagee's duties in respect of obtaining 70-81
        building societies, sales by 70-71
        other mortgagees, sales by 71-73
    purchaser, position of 81-82
    sureties, mortgagee's duties towards 76-77
    timing of sale, mortgagee's duties in respect of 73-76
Social security payments to mortgagee 23-24
Spouse of mortgagor, rights of:
    Matrimonial Homes Act 1983, as party to the action under 16-17
    See also *Co-ownership, beneficial, effect of on mortgagee*
Subrogation of subsequent mortgagees 55

Tacking of further advances 102-105
    agreement of intervening mortgagee 103
    no notice of intervening mortgages 103-104
    obligation to make a further advance 104
    registered land, in respect of 105
    See also *Priorities of mortgages*
Tenancies, effect of on mortgagee 30-36
    leases created before the mortgage 31-33
        equitable leases 31-32
        estoppel, tenancies by 32
        legal leases 31

INDEX

subsequent mortgages 32-33
leases created subsequent to the mortgage 33-36
   authorised tenancies 35-36
   unauthorised tenancies 29, 33-35
Third party rights 30-61
   co-owners, beneficial, effect of on mortgagee 36-61
   acquisition of a beneficial interest 37-49
   priority of rights 50-61
tenancies, effect of on mortgagee 30-36
   leases created before the mortgage 31-33
   leases created subsequent to the mortgage 33-36

Unauthorised tenancies, adoption by mortgagee of 29, 34-35

Commercial and Company Law

Tolley's Company Law (looseleaf)

The highly successful Tolley's Company Law is published in looseleaf format to ensure a quick and accurate service covering changes resulting from legislation, case law and the directives issuing from Europe as they occur. The emphasis of this practical service is on how the law operates on a day-to-day basis. Supplements comprise complete chapters only to facilitate quick and easy updating. Updates invoiced separately

£135.00

Tolley's Commercial Loan Agreements

James Lingard LLB, Solicitor (Norton Rose)

This book discusses the major issues likely to arise in negotiating a Loan or Multiple Option Facility Agreement. The consequences of the reforms introduced by the Companies Act 1989 and the Insolvency Act 1986 are examined.
136 pages
ISBN 0 85459 453-1
Hardback **£29.95**

Tolley's Practical Guide to Company Acquisitions (Second Edition)

A practical guide to acquisitions, covering acquisition strategy and tactics, legal aspects, tax planning, accounting requirements, employment responsibilities and pension schemes.
240 pages
ISBN 0 85459 510-4 **£29.95**

Tolley's Companies Handbook

This guide is written by the same team of experts as Tolley's much acclaimed annual reference guides and includes all legislative changes up to and including the Companies Act 1989 together with subsequent statutory instruments and latest case law. Other sources including the Admission of Securities to Listing (Yellow Book) and the City Code on Takeovers are also covered. There is also a short chapter summarising the EC legislation.
592 pages
ISBN 0 85459 581-3
£25.95

Tolley's Corporate Insolvency Handbook

Shashi Rajani, Solicitor and Keith Gregory, MA, Solicitor (Cameron Markby Hewitt)

This very practical handbook provides the law and tax position for all those involved in corporate insolvency procedures.
512 pages
ISBN 0 85459 509-0 **£27.95**

Tolley

Tolley's Journals

Taxation
Founded in 1927, *Taxation* is the only weekly tax magazine for the professional. It contains leading and feature articles on major items of interest, a news digest section, reports of tax cases, and, of course, the ever-popular readers' queries section.

Pensions World
Established since 1972, Pensions World is widely regarded as the authoritative monthly for all those involved in pensions planning. Accepted by the National Association of Pension Funds Ltd, it is distributed to all members as the Association's official journal.

Health and Safety at Work
This is the leading journal covering the health and safety scene in depth. It provides the industry with authoritative information on health and safety and environmental matters in the factory, office or on site.

Tolley's Immigration & Nationality Law & Practice
The only journal in the UK devoted exclusively to immigration and nationality law, it provides a quarterly service for immigration law practitioners wishing to keep abreast of developments in this field.

Tolley's Insurance Law & Practice
This quarterly journal publishes information on all aspects of insurance law, including regulation of insurance business, the contents of the insurance contract and the role of insurance intermediaries.

Tolley's Journal of Child Law
A specialist journal in child law for all those with a practical concern in the subject. Published quarterly, it contains articles of concern to barristers, solicitors, social workers and others working in this immensely important area of law.

Tolley's Insolvency Law & Practice
Published bi-monthly, the journal is an unrivalled forum for commentary and analysis on all areas of insolvency law. It covers case law relevant to insolvency, including unreported cases in addition to substantive articles with in-depth analysis.

Tolley's Professional Negligence
This quarterly journal provides commentary and analysis on all areas of professional liability, ethics and discipline. It is essential reading for all those practising in law, medicine, accountancy, banking, insurance, building and surveying.

Tolley's Computer Law & Practice
The leading computer law journal, it deals exclusively with the variety of legal issues arising out of the development of computer and communications technology. The journal is published six times a year.

Tolley's Trust Law International
Essential reading for every professional adviser dealing with any of the trusts used in modern practice: pensions, charities, unit trusts, banks and other trusts, and family trusts and estates. The journal is published quarterly.

Tolley's Journal of Media Law & Practice
This quarterly journal provides wide international legal coverage from around the world on broadcasting, cable and satellite, press freedom, libel, obscenity, preforming rights, copyright, privacy, recorded music and freedom of information.

Tolley's Journal of International Franchising & Distribution Law
This quarterly journal is the leading journal of its kind and is essential reading for every practitioner engaged in franchise law and practice.

For sample copies or information please ring 081-686 0115

Any new subscribers cancelling their subscriptions to Tolley periodicals within eight weeks will obtain a full refund.

Commercial and Company Law

Tolley's Business Administration (looseleaf)

The role of a company secretary can be very diverse, often being called upon to administer business affairs within a broad framework from employment to pensions and even taxation.

This title aims to cover these broad aspects while retaining information on the basic legal requirements. Specifically designed to meet the need for a highly practical and accessible reference, this convenient guide, in looseleaf format, covers a wide range of subjects, giving special consideration to their day-to-day application.

Written in plain, jargon-free language, with checklists throughout for ease of reference, this useful manual is ideal for Company Secretaries and business administrators, and all those involved with the day to day running of a company
£95.00
Updates invoiced separately

Tolley's Health and Safety at Work Handbook 1993

Malcolm Dewis LLB MIOSH
Published in association with the Royal Society for the Prevention of Accidents. Now published annually, this comprehensive handbook provides practical advice on compliance with the law and incorporates all the legislative changes and developments in practice.
790 pages approx
ISBN 0 85459 639-9 **£46.95**

Tolley's Taxation in Corporate Insolvency (Second Edition)

Anthony C R Davis MA FTII Solicitor
This is a practical guide to the taxation aspects of companies in liquidation, receivership or administration or those making voluntary arrangements. The book explains the position of the Crown, the shareholders and creditors when a company becomes insolvent and the effect of appointing an administrative receiver, an administrator or liquidator. The tax planning aspects are also covered.
288 pages
ISBN 0 85459 536-8 **£29.95**

Tolley's Company Secretary's Handbook (Second Edition)

G W Hopkinson FCIS (KPMG Peat Marwick)
This new title provides a concise, explanatory guide to the legal obligations imposed on company secretaries.

Fully up to date, the book includes the latest provisions of the Companies Act 1989 and covers such diverse areas as maintaining a company's statutory records, or implementing changes in capital structure.

Where relevant, the book contains useful precedents cross-referenced to the text. These appear at the end of the appropriate chapter and are designed to help the processing of procedures efficiently and accurately.
450 pages approx
ISBN 0 85459 679-8 **£26.95**

Tolley

Tolley Publications

TAXATION PUBLICATIONS
Tax Reference Annuals
Tolley's Income Tax 1992-93 £27.95
Tolley's Corporation Tax 1992-93 £23.95
Tolley's Capital Gains Tax 1992-93 £24.95
Tolley's Inheritance Tax 1992-93 £21.95
Tolley's Value Added Tax 1992-93 £24.95
Tolley's National Insurance Contributions 1992-93 £29.95

Tolley's Tax Legislation Series
Income Tax, Corporation Tax and Capital Gains Tax Legislation 1992-93 (2 volumes) £29.95
Inheritance Tax Legislation 1992-93 £13.95
Value Added Tax Legislation 1992-93 £19.95
NIC Legislation 1992-93 £19.95

Tolley's Looseleaf Tax Service
Tolley's Tax Service Income Tax, Corporation Tax and Capital Gains Tax (4 binders) £450.00
Tolley's Inheritance Tax Service £120.00
Tolley's Value Added Tax Service (2 binders) £325.00

Other Annual Tax Books
Tolley's Taxwise No. I 1992-93 (IT/CT/CGT) £22.95
Tolley's Taxwise No. II 1992-93 (IHT/VAT/Trusts/Tax Planning) £21.95
Tolley's Capital Allowances 1992-93 £27.95
Tolley's Estate Planning 1993 £27.95
Tolley's Official Tax Statements 1992-93 £32.95
Tolley's Tax Cases 1992 £28.95
Tolley's Tax Computations 1992-93 £31.95
Tolley's Tax Data 1992-93 £12.95
Tolley's Tax Guide 1992-93 £22.95
Tolley's Tax Office Directory 1992 £7.95
Tolley's Tax Planning 1993 (2 volumes) £60.00
Tolley's Tax Tables 1992-93 £8.95
Tolley's Taxation in the Channel Islands and Isle of Man 1992-93 £21.95
Tolley's Taxation in the Republic of Ireland 1992-93 £21.95
Tolley's VAT Planning 1993 £29.95
Tolley's VAT Cases 1992 £55.00
Tolley's Personal Tax and Investment Planning 1992-93 £28.95

Other Tax Books
Tolley's Tax Appeals to the Commissioners £14.95
Tolley's Anti-Avoidance Provisions 2nd Edition £44.95
Tolley's Tax Planning for Private Residences £29.95
Tolley's Taxation of Offshore Trusts and Funds £39.95
Tolley's Taxes Management Provisions £24.95
Tolley's Property Taxes 1992-93 £32.95
Tolley's Roll-over, Hold-over and Retirement Reliefs 2nd Edition £34.95
Tolley's Taxation of Employments £29.95
Tolley's Stamp Duties and Stamp Duty Reserve Tax £16.95
Expat Investor's Working and Retiring Abroad £9.95
Tolley's Trading in Europe £42.95
Tolley's International Tax Planning 2nd Edition (2 volumes) £85.00
Tolley's Tax Compliance and Investigations 3rd Edition £34.95
Tolley's Tax Planning for New Businesses 3rd Edition £15.95
Tolley's UK Taxation of Trusts 3rd Edition £29.95

Tolley's Benefits in Kind £5.95
Tolley's Indemnities and Warranties £34.95
Tolley's Taxation of Lloyd's Underwriters 3rd Edition £49.95
Tolley's VAT Compliance and Investigations 2nd Edition £22.95
Tolley's VAT on Construction, Land and Property 2nd Edition £23.95
Tolley's Purchase and Sale of a Private Company's Shares 4th Edition £24.95
Tolley's Taxation in Corporate Insolvency 2nd Edition £29.95
Tolley's Interest and Penalty Provisions £29.95
Tolley's Partnership Taxation £29.95
Tolley's Companies Purchasing Their Own Shares £tba
Tolley's Tax Planning for Post-Death Variations £tba
Tolley's Taxation of Trades and Professions £29.95
Tolley's Tax Planning for Family Companies £tba

LEGAL PUBLICATIONS
Tolley's Company Law (looseleaf) £135.00
Tolley's Business Administration (looseleaf) £95.00
Tolley's Index to Companies Legislation £9.95
Tolley's Practical Guide to Company Acquisitions 2nd Edition £29.95
Tolley's Company Secretary's Handbook 2nd Edition £26.95
Tolley's Directors Handbook £24.95
Tolley's Companies Handbook £25.95
Tolley's Medical Negligence £45.00
Tolley's Employment Handbook 7th Edition £22.95
Tolley's Drafting Contracts of Employment 2nd Edition £tba
Tolley's Health and Safety at Work Handbook 1993 £46.95
Tolley's Social Security and State Benefits 1992-93 £32.95
Tolley's Guide to Statutory Sick Pay and Statutory Maternity Pay 2nd Edition £24.95
Tolley's Discrimination Law Handbook £19.95
Tolley's Employment Law £tba
Tolley's Personnel Procedures £tba
Tolley's Control of Chemicals at Work £19.95
Tolley's Environmental Handbook £tba
Tolley's Child Care Law £24.95
Tolley's Commercial Loan Agreements £29.95

ACCOUNTANCY AND BUSINESS PUBLICATIONS
Tolley's Charities Manual (looseleaf) £80.00
Tolley's Manual of Accounting volume one £29.95
Tolley's Manual of Accounting volume two £19.95
Tolley's Manual of Accounting volume three £29.95
Tolley's Companies Accounts Check List 1992 £13.50 per pack of 5 (inc VAT)
Tolley's Accounting for Pension Costs £22.95
Tolley's Payroll Handbook 1993 £37.95
Tolley's Administration of Small Self-Administered Pension Schemes £29.95
Pensions Handbook £39.95
Tolley's Survey of Employee Benefits £45.00
Survey of Company Car Schemes 1992-93 £45.00

Please note: while every effort is made to ensure accuracy, information shown above is often compiled in advance of publication, and prices are subject to change without notice.

Order form

To: Tolley Publishing Company Ltd., Tolley House, 2 Addiscombe Road, Croydon, Surrey CR9 5AF England. **Telephone: 081-686 9141**

Please send me the following book(s), as shown below. I understand that if, for any reason, I am not satisfied with my order and return the book(s) in saleable condition within 21 days, Tolley will refund my money in full.

If you wish to place a standing order for any book(s) and obtain the benefits of the Tolley Subscriber Service, please tick the relevant standing order box(es). All books placed on standing order are sent post-free within the U.K. Please add 5% towards postage and packing if not placed on standing order.

Title	Price per copy	No. of copies	Standing order	Amount £
			☐	
			☐	
			☐	
			☐	
			☐	
			☐	

Plus VAT (if applicable) _____

Plus 5% postage and packing (if applicable) _____

Total £ _____

Cheque is enclosed for total amount of order £ _____
Please debit Access/Visa* account number

[_____] Access VISA   Signature _____

*Please delete as necessary

Please send me a copy of the full Tolley catalogue ☐

Name† _____

Firm _____

Position _____

Address† _____

_____

_____ Post Code _____

Telephone No _____ Date _____
†If paying by credit card, please enter name and address of cardholder

Registered No. 729731 England VAT No. 243 3583 67   Code 262

Tolley

Tax Planning

Tolley's Tax Planning 1993
Glyn Saunders MA
The thirteenth edition of this outstanding work pin-points clear, practical taxation strategies across the whole range of financial decision-making required of individuals, partnerships and corporate bodies, and is an invaluable source of ideas and advice on keeping tax payments to a minimum.
The emphasis throughout is on clear explanations and practical solutions whilst the clear format, comprehensive tables and exhaustive index give you immediate access to essential information.
1,600 pages approx (Two volumes)
ISBN 0 85459 646-1 **£60.00**

Tolley's Estate Planning 1993
Written by Price Waterhouse, this detailed and comprehensive guide covers every aspect of estate planning in a clear and readable style, and is full of practical planning suggestions.
This fifth edition covers three main areas of concern – lifetime planning, will and post-death planning, and international aspects providing detailed guidance on this complex subject.
The fifth edition has been fully revised and updated to include all of the changes made by the Finance (No 2) Act 1992 including the taxation of overseas resident settlements.
400 pages approx
ISBN 0 85459 645-3 **£27.50**

Tolley's VAT Planning 1993
Patrick Noakes MA FCA ATII
The eighth edition of this important work is an invaluable source of ideas and advice on achieving the optimum tax position, thereby preventing unnecessary VAT liabilities and avoiding the many pitfalls of this complicated tax.
Comprising 20 chapters of clear, explanatory text, each written by a practising VAT expert, this practical guide has been fully updated to include all the changes introduced by relevant legislation and case law, including that of the European Community as well as the United Kingdom.
Covering a wide range of areas including registration, partial exemption, international services and business expenses, this book will prove indispensable not only to accountants, lawyers and other practitioners advising on VAT planning, but also to corporate and non-corporate businesses with an interest in minimising VAT liabilities.
570 pages approx
ISBN 0 85459 642-9 **£29.95**

Tolley's Tax Planning for Private Residences
Matthew Hutton MA(Oxon) FTII
This book brings together the planning considerations for all the taxes which affect private residences in one easy-to-use source.
The text adopts a practical, problem solving approach and uses numerous worked examples to illustrate the points which need to be taken into account.
Contents:
● Introduction ● Capital Gains Tax: the relief and restrictions; some computational aspects ● Inheritance Tax Mitigations: lifetime giving; will and post-death planning ● Income tax relief for loan interest
248 pages
ISBN 0 85459 584-8 **£29.95**

Tolley